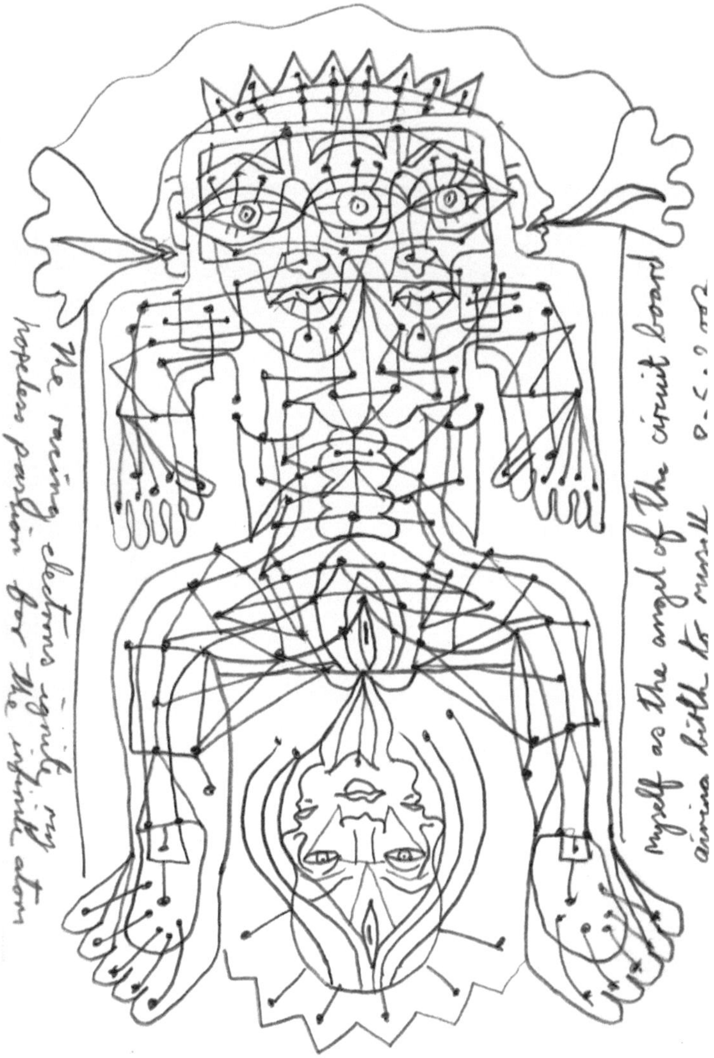

Art by Val Denham

Outsider Inpatient

Reflections on Art as Therapy

Edited by

Elisabeth Punzi
Vanessa Sinclair

TRAPARTbooks

GÖTEBORGS UNIVERSITET

Outsider Inpatient: Reflections on Art as Therapy
Trapart Books 2021

In cooperation with The Center for Critical Heritage Studies (CCHS) and the University of Gothenburg

ISBN 978-91-986243-8-0

Trapart Books
P.O. Box 8105
SE-104 20 Stockholm
Sweden

info@trapart.net
www.trapart.net

Outsider Inpatient: Contents

Art by Val Denham

Editor's Introduction

Elizabeth Punzi

In April 2018, Inez Edström, Stefan Karlsson and I, along with several artists, arranged a guided tour at Lillhagen, a former psychiatric hospital located just outside Gothenburg, Sweden. This event was realized through my work at the Center for Critical Heritage Studies (CCHS) at Gothenburg University and University College London. Most often, my work at CCHS is focused on the heritage of marginalized individuals and those who have been deemed deviant at any given point in time. In organizing such an event, Inez, Stefan and I wished to acknowledge and share the murals former patients[1] had created in the basement of the hospital during the last decades of the 20th century. It should be noted that the patients were paid to decorate the walls of the basement, and accordingly, these paintings of the patients were considered valuable.

In our current day and age, however, mental health care buildings are often quite sterile and are presented as perfectly and optimally designed. As such, they are delivered to patients and clinicians, who in turn have nothing to add. Neither patients nor clinicians are permitted to leave traces of any kind nor are they encouraged to show anything of themselves. I consider it important to illustrate that there was a time, not so long ago, when patients could leave traces of themselves, and I organized this event at Lillhagen in order to highlight this. I don't mean to idealize or romanticize the past. Past psychiatric care was certainly horrendous in many ways. But that being said, it could be argued that mental health care is in many ways even more totalitarian now. The power of yesterday's authoritarian structure was obvious. Today the underlying power structure is clearly present but may be even more insidious, disguised in so called anti-stigma campaigns, and admonishing architecture that is said to be healing, while assertive outreach teams go into people's homes to medicate them. In many ways this has made the power structures even more difficult to combat, as obvious power could be protested against, from without as well as from within. Practitioners and patients could create a counterculture (as in the Democratic psychiatry movement in Italy), express criticism through artistic work, and develop non-medical approaches.

The guided tour of Lillhagen was ultimately a huge success, and I learned a lot

1 The word "patient" is used to describe the position of those individuals who were inmates at Lillhagen and has nothing to do with a medicalized perspective.

through the creation of this event. But the organization of such an event was full of obstacles, and it felt like a catastrophe at times. The intense level of sensationalism that surrounds old psychiatric buildings as well as psychiatrized individuals quickly became clear to me. This emotional charge and apparent ambivalence likely contributed to the hype. Hundreds of people expressed their desire to be part of the event, which was wonderful, however, there was only room for seventy people, and those who were not able to take part in the event acted out in a variety of ways. I was accused of discrimination, and some went to extreme measures in attempting to force me to include them. Some people announced that they would participate in the event anyway, and I was even threatened a couple of times. We had to hire guards to protect the arrangement and to ensure the peacefulness of a home for the elderly in the area.

In hindsight, I should have been prepared for this. People seem obsessed with the idea that there is another van Gogh to be discovered whenever psychiatrized individuals engage in creative expressions. As if you need to be some kind of genius in order to be valued and encouraged to express yourself through art, poetry, drama, or music, not that many seemed to recognize van Gogh's talent in his lifetime. I hope I did not contribute to maintaining sensationalism and othering of psychiatrized individuals through hosting this event. My goal was to bring this beautiful work to light and illustrate the importance of the creative process itself.

Importantly, I must note that no former patients nor mental health care users behaved in this way. Those who were most obtrusive and/or aggressive were established practitioners, who seemed to feel left out. I can understand why people wished to participate. We had insightful and illustrative talks by Per Magnus Johansson, Johannes Nordholm, and Christian Munthe, who reflected on the arbitrariness of psychiatric diagnoses, what it means to be human, the importance of art, and how we as human beings express ourselves beyond words. Moreover, musicians Fågelle and Henryk Lipp performed and created a sound installation which included quotes from former patients. And of course, without the guided tour, this book would not have been realized.

I also met people who I would never have met otherwise. Individuals who are thoughtful and hoped to preserve the murals and create remembrance of former patients. Many people approached me at the event and thanked me for acknowledging Lillhagen and the former patients. Several shared their own memories and experiences with me. Some had worked there, others had relatives who had been patients there. Still others had themselves been patients at Lillhagen. They shared examples of oppression, but also shared stories of connectedness and support, and of experiences of having felt "seen" as individuals. Some former patients described how occupational therapists had supported them in engaging in handicraft, which meant a lot to them, how important the hairdresser at the hospital area had been for their recovery, and how the patients supported one other.

Lillhagen is now being transformed to a residential area called Lillhagen Park. One benefit of the overwhelming response in the media to our event in 2018, is that the hype contributed to the politically governed decision to name one street in

Lillhagen Park, "Kulvertkonstens Väg" (roughly translated to "the street of the basement art"). This is especially gratifying in light of the global tendency to disregard the material as well as the immaterial heritage of psychiatry. Buildings are frequently demolished or, if they are considered valuable real estate, rebuilt as business parks, SPA facilities, or residential areas. The buildings may remain, but the traces of their past are often obliterated, or turned into sensationalized selling points for wealthy investors. The redevelopment of these institutions is part of broader neoliberal trajectories of displacement, gentrification and privatization in which individuals that are considered deviant become excluded.

If any heritage of the building or site remains, it is the heritage of the patients, and Mad people's history, that is most especially excluded, while doctors, architects who planned the buildings, and sometimes nurses, are memorialized with plaques and provided with the opportunity to portray the field of psychiatry and the lives of the patients in books and in museums. In such museums and books, the mainstream narrative dispenses the idea of constant progress, with previous psychiatric care depicted as inhumane and unscientific, while current practices are considered humane, effective, and to the highest standard of scientific research. These narratives serve to justify current practices and thus contribute to the occlusion of ongoing injustices. They also espouse the idea of consistent progress, as though we live in an era of scientific breakthroughs with no need to look back, or sideways. I would like to argue that we need to consider Mad people's heritage, integrate the patients' perspectives, and think more carefully about which parts of psychiatry should be acknowledged and preserved. We also need to ask ourselves what current practices are remnants of oppressive historical practices and perspectives, and what can we learn from prior practices and activities that challenged mentalist ideas and/or were established through the counterculture of Mad people?

Finally, I would like to thank Dan Hansson and Michael "Micke" Petersson who work at Lokalförvaltningen, the organization that owns the buildings, including the basement, at Lillhagen. Without them the tour would never had been realized.

March 2021

In the beginning was not the word

Per Magnus Johansson

In the beginning was not the word, but the deed. "Im Anfang war die Tat," wrote Johann Wolfgang von Goethe (1749-1832). The phrase is quoted by Sigmund Freud (1856-1939) in *Totem and Taboo*, 1912-1913. In the beginning was not the word. In the beginning was the deed, but not only the deed, there was also, and not least, the image. In the beginning was speechlessness. The human being, that is the newly born infant, does not react exclusively to words, but also to images perceived by the eye. Nor does the small child express itself with the aid of what he or she will come to recognize and denote as words. Speechlessness, the silence that reigns when there are no words, and the image, make up the original point of departure in the life of the human being. The French historian of ideas Michel Foucault (1926-1984) maintained that Sigmund Freud marked the paradigmatic break between the diagnostics of the eye and the ear; the doctor – before Freud – could by the power of his autocratic medical gaze define and analyse the suffering subject; the madman was subjected to the penetrating gaze of the doctor. And the doctor can still do this today.

In the late 19th century Freud introduced the now famous couch; the work instrument that allows the patient to speak while lying down. This meant that the analyst and the patient no longer looked at each other, did not stare into each other's eyes; instead, a dialectic between speech and listening developed in the therapeutic room. With the support of the French psychoanalytic tradition, one could say that psychoanalysis came to comprise – and still comprises – the translation of imaginary ideas – not seldom images – into words; in other words; from images to words. From old words to new words. How can I speak about what I have seen? And later, how can I speak about what I have heard? Images and words, words and images. Images become words, words become images. Words create new words, and stories get new colours. Words generate new images. The movement between images and words, and between words and images, is practically never-ending.

Freud was no stranger to analysing images. In his model for analysing cultural phenomena – apparent in the work *Leonardo da Vinci, A Memory of his Childhood* – he utilized the analysis of images as well as the analysis of words. In the book about Leonardo da Vinci (1452-1519), published in 1910, Freud analysed Leonardo's notebook and diary, as well as his paintings "Mona Lisa" and "The Virgin and Child with Saint Anne." Freud's commentary to the texts is supplemented with the analyses of the paintings. His conclusion suggests that Leonardo da Vinci had the capacity to express the innermost part of himself – his desire, his longing, his fear, his lack, sorrow, and despair – in his diary and his notebook as well as in his paintings, in images.

From a certain point of view one can see Leonardo's paintings as expressions of his reworking of certain images, the silence and the speechlessness that tormented him, yet the paintings are also, according to Freud, in another sense, expressions of the fact that Leonardo overcame what could have become his captivity, his introversion, or what one with the aid of a psychiatric diagnosis could call his autism; or with the aid of a neurological diagnosis could call his aphasia. He started to speak – with images – from himself to all of us; to all those who lived in his time, to those who were dead, and to those who still had not been born.

It is no coincidence that the two great Swedish artists Ernst Josephson (1851-1906) and Carl Fredrik Hill (1849-1911) have attracted much interest among psychiatrists, psychoanalysts and psychologists. How can one understand the fact that the anguished and psychically suffering individual is capable of artistic feats, not to speak of artistic genius? For long periods of their lives, these two artists had an indomitable will to express themselves and an inner life which, as I remarked on briefly earlier, was characterized by desire, longing, sadness, hatred, fear and lack. The previously mentioned Michel Foucault has pointed out that it is impossible to ever completely capture the mystery of artistic creativity with the aid of psychiatric diagnoses and discourse, or, as Freud put it long before this, namely in 1928: "Before the problem of artistic creativity analysis must, alas, lay down its arms." However, this never hindered Freud from trying to reveal the possible connections between on the one hand the origin and history of the artist, and on the other hand the artist's work. Psychoanalysis can illuminate complex relations, but it cannot answer the question of why an individual artist was able to access his or her creative ability.

Obviously, not everyone who works with images has the same stature in the history of art as Leonardo da Vinci, Carl Fredrik Hill, or Ernst Josephson. Furthermore, it is not my task as a psychoanalyst and historian of ideas to decide who does nor does not belong to art history. This task is more suited to an art historian, for instance the here present Johannes Nordholm. What I do feel more inclined to speak about is concerned with the inner need of the individual to tell his or her own story. This universal need is inscribed in human nature and is uncompromising.

We survive by being permitted to create a narrative about what is most urgent. If that narrative is to become meaningful to communicate to others, there must be a place. A museum, a lecture hall, a school room, a library, a psychoanalyst's room, a studio, a restaurant, a bar, or a culvert. In these places – and perhaps in others as well – there also must be a perceptive eye or a sensitive ear, or in the ideal situation, both open eyes as well as attentively listening ears. This is also a perspective from which we can view the paintings that are on display here, in other words, we can see them as expressions of the desire of the individual human being to be seen and heard. It is more than essential that society preserves these places.

Nor shall we ever forget that some of those who both claimed and received a place in the culvert also were denied a place in another context. Without a place, there is no life. The place constitutes the prerequisite for meeting the other, as well as – and not least importantly – a fragment of oneself. Or expressed in another way, a place comes to life where the suffering subject, as the poet Gunnar Ekelöf (1907-1968) writes in *Sagan om Fatumeh* ("The Tale of Fatumeh") from 1966, can say to the other: "Speak to my heart."

The asylum of art
– Visions of vitality in the culvert at Lillhagen Hospital

Johannes Nordholm

Art is contextual. Seeing the murals painted by psychiatric patients in the culvert at Lillhagen hospital is a unique experience. It is different from seeing them in any other setting. To encounter them in the abandoned subterranean passage, in a bleak, slightly jarring light, surrounded by stale air and walls patinated by decades of exposure in a hospital thoroughfare, is almost a kind of shock. Suddenly, there is life. Figures spring forth from the walls, and landscapes appear, with trees, flowers and animals. It makes one think of what it must have been like when the remains of Pompeii, buried by the eruption of Vesuvius in A.D. 79, were rediscovered in the mid-18th century. They were first revealed by the architect Domenico Fontana in the late 16th century, but were then forgotten for around 150 years, until excavations resumed under the Neapolitan ruler Charles of Bourbon. To dig up a practically intact Roman city, with its frescoes, statuary and architecture, must have been awe-inspiring. Other examples of this kind of discovery are perhaps when modern man laid eyes on the cave paintings in Lascaux or Altamira. Another age comes to life, thanks to the miraculous preservation of its artworks in their original environment.

The Pompeiians painted frescoes to embellish their homes, and prehistoric man presumably used art in religious ceremonies connected to hunting. Creating beauty and appeasing the gods are part of the origins of art. Why did the patients at Lillhagen Hospital create art? Was it for the same reasons, or are the reasons different due to the psychiatric context? The connection between psychic suffering and creativity is part of Western culture since antiquity. In the dialogue Ion, the Greek philosopher Plato (5th-4th century B.C.) views creativity as a kind of divine madness. He was sceptical of the artist's capacity for mimesis, the imitation of reality, because it did not necessarily convey the truth. Plato was deeply concerned with the question of truth, a specific kind of truth. Why would an artist diverge from the truth? Or, to put it in another way, what is the difference between art and philosophy?

Art and loss

In Greek mythology, the poet Orpheus loses his lover Eurydice to a snake bite. Overcome with grief, he sings and creates poetry. From his longing for his lost lover, a flow of creativity pours forth. His artistry is such that it placates the guardians of the underworld and allows him to retrieve Eurydice. He is allowed to bring her back from Hades to the world of the living on one condition: he must not turn around as they walk toward the surface. We can picture them on their ascent. She walks behind him, holding a certain distance, and as they proceed he starts to wonder, is she really there? Or has she been left behind, has she disappeared? He cannot stand the uncertainty, and he longs for her so much that he turns around. In a fleeting moment he sees her, then she is gone. She was there, but now she must irrevocably return to the realm of the dead. Back in the living world, the bereaved Orpheus continues to sing, in a poetic outpouring that is conditioned by the fact that he has lost his beloved forever. The French author Maurice Blanchot (1907-2003) writes that Orpheus' glance is predetermined by the transgressive nature of his expedition to retrieve her, facilitated by his artistic talent; his desire does not respect the laws of life and death. Thus, it is no surprise that he cannot respect the rule that he is not allowed to turn around. His desire for Eurydice is so intense – he must see her, touch her, at all costs – that he is predestined to lose her. But this is also the reason why he can create.

Sigmund Freud (1856-1939), the father of psychoanalysis, compares the creativity of the artist, without disrespect, to the play and day-dreaming of the child. Unconscious wishes and erotic drives are present, and the recourse to fantasy is connected to the fact that there is a gap between what the individual desires and what reality has to offer. "We may lay it down that a happy person never phantasies, only a dissatisfied one."[1] There is a kinship between Freud's view and the Orpheus myth. The desire for something which is not present in real life calls up the powers of the imagination. Freud noted that most individuals are loath to reveal their fantasies or day-dreams, but thanks to the psychoanalytic method, his troubled patients disclosed theirs to him. However, for Freud, the difference between being healthy and being ill was not a dichotomy, rather a graded scale. He saw similarities between supposedly ill and supposedly healthy individuals; the same principles of psychic life were operational. He writes that he "found good reason to suppose that our patients tell us nothing that we might not also hear from healthy people."[2]

The psychiatric patient as artist

Freud's openness to his patients' fantasies and inner worlds is mirrored in the increased interest in the artworks of psychiatric patients in the decades around 1900. In the late 19th century, the connection between psychic suffering and creativity came into focus, in part due to the posthumous fame of the Dutch painter Vincent van Gogh (1853-1890), whose troubled life became a kind of founding myth for modernism. Late in his career, without having achieved any public success, van Gogh was institutionalised after a serious psychotic episode. In European culture, irrationality and madness became the subject of study. Starting from artists who also were psychiatric patients, art historians and psychiatrists became interested in

1 Freud, Sigmund. "Creative Writers and Day-Dreaming", 1908.
2 Freud, 1908.

psychiatric patients who also were artists. What distinguished their creativity, could their artworks be appreciated as art, and what could be learnt from them?

In his doctoral thesis from 2002, *Särlingskap och konstnärsmyt*, (*Being an Outsider and the Artist Myth*) Per Dahlström (b. 1957), a curator at the Gothenburg Museum of Art, studies the question of outsider art in the context of modernism and the changes in society and culture in the early 20th century. For him, the recognition of outsider art has its roots in the presumed connection between psychic suffering and creativity. He traces an evolution that passes via the intermediate figure of the bohemian, a hero in 20th century culture epitomised by the poets Charles Baudelaire (1821-1867), Hans Jaeger (1854-1910) and Alfred Jarry (1873-1907), who stood outside of the bourgeoise establishment. However, the bohemians were still clearly within the art institution, that is, their art was recognized and included, in contrast with the situation of the outsider, who was outside of both society and the art institution. The archetypical examples of the outsider in this context are the child, the psychiatric patient, and the so-called primitive. In the history of ideas, modernism in art is seen as a reaction to a technological and bureaucratic civilisation that alienated humanity from her true instincts and expressions. The outsider, in contrast, was uncorrupted by socialisation and the demands of civilisation, and thus still in contact with authentic drives and emotions. The turn from illusionistic and technically refined modes of visual expression to stylised, distorted and exaggerated idioms can be credited to the cult of authenticity; the modernist style was considered more direct and unfiltered, and therefore more truthful.

Three pioneers: Réja, Morgenthaler and Prinzhorn

Dahlström lays out the theoretical foundations for modernism's cult of the outsider by summarising three ground-breaking works, *L'Art chez les Fous: Le Dessin, La Prose, La Poésie* (1907) by Marcel Réja (a pseudonym for the psychiatrist Paul Meunier, 1873-1957), *Ein Geisteskranker als Künstler: Adolf Wölfli* (1921) by the psychiatrist Walter Morgenthaler (1882-1965), and *Bildnerei des Geisteskranke. Ein Beitrag zur Psychologie unde Psychopathologie des Gestaltung* (1922) by the psychiatrist Hans Prinzhorn (1886-1933). Based on their clinical contacts with patients, these medical doctors and specialists in psychiatry who also were schooled in art history attempted to add to the knowledge not only about psychiatric illness but also about the essence of art. Broadly speaking, they analyse the creative output of patients and, in principle, attribute to them the status of art. In addition, they perceive qualities in them that are not present in professional art and arguably contribute to clarifying the nature of artistic creativity. They were philosophically indebted to the era's investigators of deep psychology, chiefly the aforementioned Sigmund Freud, Carl Gustaf Jung (1875-1961) and Otto Gross (1877-1920). Based on the Freudian discovery, all three were interested in the irrational elements of patients' speech, dreams, actions and creative feats, and developed theories to understand their meaning. All three acknowledged that unconscious processes were at play in art, but their positions also diverge. Freud did not embrace the concept of universal meanings in unconscious

expressions (for instance, the symbolic meaning of objects in a dream). Jung, on the other hand, with his concept of the collective unconscious, maintained that artists tap into a reserve of meaning that is common to all of mankind, irrespective of culture, upbringing and other individual factors. Gross was perhaps the most radical of the three, a bohemian who, though a medical doctor, was addicted to narcotics and had an anarchistic life-style, at times living in the both celebrated and notorious artist colony in Ascona in Switzerland. Gross reversed the roles of the patient and the so-called normal person, considering the madman healthy, and the conventional citizen mad. He viewed the patriarchal family as oppressive of human nature, and advocated matriarchy and sexual freedom. Deviant art was for Gross a means of emancipation from the shackles of bourgeoise society.

Let us return to the works by Réja, Morgenthaler and Prinzhorn, about art by psychiatric patients. Réja studied both visual art and writing by psychiatric patients in France. He rejected the idea of a link between psychic suffering and creativity but suggested that the art of the patients was more subjective, and less dictated by conventions, than the art of professional artists, and thus more in line with the new artistic ideals of the time.

Morgenthaler analysed the paintings of a single patient, Adolf Wölfli, an insane sexual offender who was highly prolific as an artist. The images of Wölfli are packed with details, rich in geometrical structures and imaginative figures, and contain numbers and texts, stemming from an irrepressible drive to communicate. Morgenthaler arrives at the conclusion that Wölfli, just as other artists, had a highly developed sense of form;[3] Wölfli understood rhythms, patterns, and the underlying laws

3 According to Dahlström, Morgenthaler was inspired by the theory of Hermann Ebbinghaus (1850-1909). Ebbinghaus described certain fundamental objectivity functions that regulate the human psyche

of proportions that give rise to aesthetic value. In this Morgenthaler found support in the statements of famous artists like Paul Cézanne and Vasily Kandinsky, who also sought to express formal principles in images that were not restricted to the superficial appearance of reality. However, Morgenthaler saw that there were different routes to adopting these principles. If the schooled artists achieved a new direction by consciously tearing down conventions, Wölfli achieved his artistic liberation due to the involuntary breakdown of parts of his mental capacity. Morgenthaler uses the comparison that both an earthquake and a builder can demolish a house – the result is the same in one respect, but there is also a difference. In Dahlström's reading, Morgenthaler considered that Wölfli expressed a deeper level of his unconscious than professional artists and tried to promote him specifically as a unique genius.

Finally, Prinzhorn collected the artworks of patients at the University Clinic in Heidelberg, were he worked as a deputy to the Head Psychiatrist. In his famous book, he presented the patients' works along with their anamneses, in a kind of illustrated case studies. Prinzhorn's true goal, however, was to understand and define human creativity. He classified the various expressions he came across in the patients' works, elucidating various intrinsic tendencies, such as to play, decorate, organise, mimic and symbolise. Ultimately, he was seeking a kind of bottom line or core in creativity, which he found in the biological impulse to personally communicate with another human being, along the lines of the philosopher Ludwig Klages' (1872-1956) thinking on graphology. Prinzhorn viewed creativity as a fundamental drive that could express itself in various ways, the simplest of which was in doodling, the kind of meaningless drawings or patterns that people who are bored during a lecture or speaking

---

and structure its perception of itself and the world. The objectivity functions were particularly strong in artists. Dahlström, p. 60.

on the phone could make. According to Dahlström, Prinzhorn concludes that the art of the patients is characterized by playfulness and symbolisation to a higher degree than conventional art. Also, it has a kind of foreign and self-sufficient character, as if written in a language of its own, that no one else understands. The word autistic is used in this context. Prinzhorn sees this as a positive quality and considers that the art of children and so-called primitive cultures displays the same characteristics. He refers to Freud's *Totem und Tabu* (1913) and its analogy between the cultural development of civilisation and the psychic development of the individual. The patient is a kind of child, somehow functioning at a lower level of sophistication, but living in an adult world, with more references and experience, which distinguishes his or her creativity from that of actual children.

Symptom or sublimation?

Prinzhorn, like Morgenthaler, upholds the idea of a connection between insanity and creativity. In his discussion on the art of the schizophrenic, he states that while being afflicted with schizophrenia does not make a person an artist, artists who are struck by the disease remain artists. The artistic powers are intact, despite schizophrenia. However, the tragic isolation due to the illness means that the artist is no longer concerned with communicating in an overtly understandable manner. The autistic element can thus paradoxically liberate an unconventional symbolising force in the patient's work. Is this introverted mode a deeper way of communicating? Does it speak more directly to the unconscious of the other? In the art of the fundamentally isolated schizophrenic, we perhaps find a creative expression of the solitude of all human beings, in my interpretation of Prinzhorn.

It is also a question whether all creative expressions by psychiatric patients are constructive. The basic position of Réja, Morgenthaler and Prinzhorn seems to be that all artworks by psychiatric patients are meaningful and represent a positive aspect, something intact and life-affirming in them. However, it is unclear why certain creative acts could not be part of psychiatric symptomatology and of questionable value to the patient or anyone else. A psychoanalytic way of formulating this question would be to ask if they are expressions of psychopathology and cause suffering, or examples of sublimation, in the Freudian tradition a constructive transformation of sexual energy that provides meaning and potentially relief.[4] Certainly, there are differences in the aesthetic quality of different artworks by psychiatric patients, from the perspective of both conventional and modernist artistic ideals. But does that matter to the patient/artist? Does it matter to the art historian or the potential public?

The outside comes inside

Artists as well were intrigued by the art of psychiatric patients in the first decades of

4 This fundamental question has been posed in the work of the psychoanalyst Ernst Kris, whose answer to the question of whether the creativity of psychiatric patients should be considered art or not is answered in the negative.

the 20th century. Among others, the artists Max Ernst, Hans Arp, Paul Klee, and the poet André Breton, the founder of surrealism, studied the artworks in Prinzhorn's book and were influenced by them.[5] Ernst, for instance, developed a regressive alter-ego in the figure of the bird Loplop. In this guise he seemed to see himself as free to transcend artistic boundaries. In art history, the most apparent heir to Réja, Morgenthaler and Prinzhorn is the French artist Jean Dubuffet (1901-1985). Dubuffet founded an art movement, L'Art Brut, which incorporated the quintessential features of the art of psychiatric patients and provided an institutional framework for outsider art. Dubuffet too was influenced by the writings of Prinzhorn. His approach, while taken to the extreme, was still connected to the mainstream of modernism in art, which ensconced the idea of the outsider as the artist par excellence. Ideally, the artist should be free of all conventions and social obligations; he should not be bound to anything. Art should only be made for its own sake. Dubuffet's belief in the creative value of spontaneity was utopian. After the 1940s, he pursued a highly successful career as an artist. Despite his ideals of independence, he became a part of the art world, and wrote influential theoretical works, by and large continuing in the tradition of Réja, Morgenthaler and Prinzhorn.

Outsider art had become an accepted part of the art world: it was now both outside and inside the art world. In a broader perspective, it was part of a shift of artistic ideals and a radical break in history that can be summed up as a revolt against naturalism and classical beauty, and the supposed normative patriarchal power embodied by these ideals. The art of psychiatric patients inspired the development of artistic styles that no longer aimed to please, but rather to express emotion, positive or negative, and which could accept a broader range of subject matter, from the abstract and decorative to starkly symbolic imagery. The aesthetic thrust of this art also aimed to overthrow conventional society, and free humanity from her captivity in civilisation. Perhaps the words of the author Birgitta Trotzig can illustrate these revolutionary claims of a primordial nature:

Outsiders in art? Not at all. On the contrary: right in the centre. Screaming in cells, meditating on rubbish heaps, mumbling, singing, crystal clear and incomprehensible, they show us purely and brutally what art (that is right, art – Art, the circus, the act, ART) really is: expressions of life in the form of images. Magic and conquering the world, the total creative gesture – all of this doomed, limited, parodical, utterly frail, straw and hay, repulsive masks, scarecrows, the idea of a human being in total captivity and limitless freedom. Every child knows what it is.[6]

Works and themes

What can be said of the works in the culvert at Lillhagen hospital, in the light of this historical overview? The context of the works' production is discussed elsewhere but would seem to be in line with the thinking of Prinzhorn and Dubuffet, with their optimistic view on the emancipatory function of the artistic practices of psychiatric

5 Dahlström, s. 68.
6 Trotzig, Birgitta. *Särlingar i konsten.*

patients. Here, the therapeutic effects of these works are not in focus. Instead, I attempt to characterize and interpret some of the artworks in the culvert. What do these artworks express, are there references to art history, and in which ways do these subterranean works display connections to the tenets of outsider art?

Artistically, they are in general marked by strong colours and simplified forms, expressing energy and vitality, but one can also discern existential themes that may be related to the artists' life situations as patients at a psychiatric institution. Some of them construct a dream landscape, a natural environment where there is openness and freedom. As in the case of the famous Gothenburg colourists, the modernist painters who were trained by the painter Tor Bjurström at the Valand Academy in the 1920s (and several of whom became psychiatric patients), colour seems to be used like an elixir of life[7] to liven up a grey and gloomy world, almost like an act of resistance.

Modernism is clearly a stylistic reference, and one can easily imagine that the patients were encouraged to follow their spontaneous creativity, without eschewing distorted or seemingly unpolished expressions. The force of the creative urge, and a tendency toward either idyllic, potentially naïve representation or abstraction seems present in most works.

The dance of life and death

In the intersection between two corridors, a larger space contains a mural which stretches across an entire wall. The scene is a restaurant or open-air café, and thirteen

7 This is an expression used by Håkan Wettre, a former curator at the Gothenburg Museum of Art, to describe the Gothenburg colourists' relationship to colour.

couples, quite ordinarily dressed, are dancing across the room, almost in a kind of procession. The pictorial space appears to be an illusionistic continuation of the real room, in the manner of Leonardo da Vinci's famous "The Last Supper" (1495-1498), on the wall of the refectory in the monastery of Santa Maria della Grazie in Milan. In fact, as a visitor to one of the guided tours of the culvert at Lillhagen Hospital in April 2018 pointed out, there are also thirteen couples in the Lillhagen fresco, corresponding to the thirteen seated figures in "The Last Supper." The style of painting is simplified but realistic and the colours are commonplace, in an idiom reminiscent of explanatory pictures in technical manuals. The scene seems controlled and static. Yet in the context, the dancing figures become moving reminders of life. Despite their aura of silence, they evoke a low-key longing for loving contact. In Greek mythology, dancing is associated with Dionysus and his female followers, the Maenads, and the affirmation of instincts, sexuality and wine-induced rapture. Without going to these excesses, the fresco at Lillhagen subtly evokes this Dionysian dimension of life, while at the same time maintaining a perhaps necessary order.

The body and eroticism

The dance continues in a painting with a resplendently blue man. Together with a woman, painted in soft skin tones, he performs a stylised dance movement. Their bodies are swathed in a suggestive yellow glow, like an aura, that imbues them with dynamism and liveliness. Their bodies are drawn to each other, but also seem to slip away. Their nudity is not erotic, rather it shows vulnerability and strength at the same time. The artist Sylwa employs a technique in which she adds light paint over darker areas, providing her figures with three-dimensional texture and energy. The blueness of the male figure is intriguing. Does it signal melancholy, in a conventional reading of the colour, or perhaps that he is an unreal figure, a memory or fantasy?

In another of her works, Sylwa paints a female nude, clearly displaying the stylistic features of modernism. The contours are simplified and slightly angular, along the lines of modernist art by artists such as Henri Matisse or Amedeo Modigliani. The face resembles sculptures from ancient Greece and Rome. The colour scale tends towards white and yellow, with green, turquoise and blue highlights, and the artist uses the underlying wall as part of the picture. The figure expresses dynamic movement and gracious elegance. The graffiti of a later date does not detract from its inherent beauty. Sometimes, beauty provokes the urge to destroy.

Symbols of life and death

In another nude study we see a woman in a red boat on a blue sea. Above the horizon there is an expanse of green sky. The formal language is simplified and the colours deep and saturated. The facial expression of the female figure reveals nothing – she resembles a figure from archaic art, with a divine presence. She holds one of her hands over the side of the boat, perhaps inviting the viewer to join her, or taking farewell. In art, the boat is often used to symbolise the journey through life from birth to death. There is also another symbol in the painting, a white bird. Birds often symbolise freedom, but in this context a chilling interpretation could be that freedom is only achieved in death. The white bird could also be the human soul, travelling toward the afterlife, as in the Swiss romantic painter Arnold Böcklin's famous painting "Toteninsel" ("The Island of Death").

In another mysterious image, which utilizes the white-painted wall as its backdrop, we see a naked woman surrounded by two green-clad figures, one of whom genuflects and presses his face towards the woman's round belly, while the other holds one hand on her shoulder and another on her hip. With a technique that utilizes white elevation contours to create volumes, a deeply symbolic yet unfathomable scene unfolds. The pregnant woman appears to be both venerated and protected by the green-clad men. Sometimes, hospital staff are clad in green. Are they protecting a symbol of life, or smothering it? The woman, in her naked state, calls to mind a stone age fertility goddess, placed in a modern context. Her facial features are stylised and accentuated so that she becomes almost a kind of feline, on the boundary between human and animal. A fascination with the biological basis of human life seems to be shown side by side with a reference to religious symbolism.

Nature myths

Animals are powerful symbols, not least the lion, here shown as a companion or guard of the lying figure, which, in the manner of mummy or ancient Greek herm, lacks arms. She seems bound in a cocoon. Is this an image of confinement, of being frozen by an interior or exterior paralysis, of being held prisoner, turned to stone, like those who looked into the eyes of the Medusa? The girl and the lion are portrayed in a landscape with billowing grass on sandy earth, perhaps a beach with grass-clad sand dunes. The picture has a diagonal movement, a clarity of colour and a rhythm in its forms that connect it to modernism. The lion seems almost human, with its forlorn demeanour. The lion is a symbolic, regal animal, which in Christian art is associated with Saint Mark and Saint Hieronymous. Here, one tends to think of the lion as a protective figure, safeguarding the defenceless girl who is perhaps wrapped up in her own struggle.

Another painting, which features a tree, sets into play a symbolism connected to Yggdrasil, the tree of life in Nordic mythology. The colour scheme is the typical four-tone of the Gothenburg colourist Ivan Ivarson: red, blue, yellow and green. Many trained artists might find the subject matter and the style of painting to be overly obvious, somehow speaking too clearly; but in the context of the culvert underneath a hospital for psychiatric patients, we experience the direct power of this kind of painting partly due to the contrast between its naïvety and the grimness of the surroundings.

The painting with two figures in green is one of the most imaginative. One of the figures holds the other's shoulders, and points towards or holds a glowing yellow globe in the purple sky. In the bodies of the figures, red structures are painted, which can be interpreted as parts of the skeleton or internal organs. This is an example of a kind of seeing which does not stay within the boundaries of ordinary seeing Nakedness and vulnerability are revealed; the inside is turned out. The artist sees the truth about the human body, a truth about its biological machine-like inner nature that most people prefer not to think about. Visually, red and green, and purple and yellow are complementary colours, reinforcing each other. The green colour symbolizes growth and life, but also sickness. The figures' relation to the sun associates them with religious art. Perhaps they indicate mankind's links to another world, or the divine sphere. Are they an example of what Prinzhorn defined as the tendency to create symbols?

Decoration and the fear of emptiness

In the culvert we also come across art of a more decorative character. Here, we can recall that Prinzhorn considered the tendency to decorate as one of mankind's primal creative urges. In a long series of decorative images, executed in a picture-perfect, shiny pictorial genre not unlike the visual idiom of 1950s advertising, we see a multitude of horns in different colours, and cornucopias, symbols of wealth and prosperity from antiquity. Essentially, the decorative array of horns is not unlike the embellishment of Roman temple. Do the symbols for music and riches refer to hopes for the future, or are they simply intended to brighten up the culvert with noisy colours?

In a black and white painting, the artist has used the style of comic book illustration, repeating certain simple motifs: a head in profile, sometimes endowed with tiny legs, like the characteristic child's drawing, and a plain but expressively drawn flower. The energy and directness call to mind graffiti or the work of an artist like the Ameri-

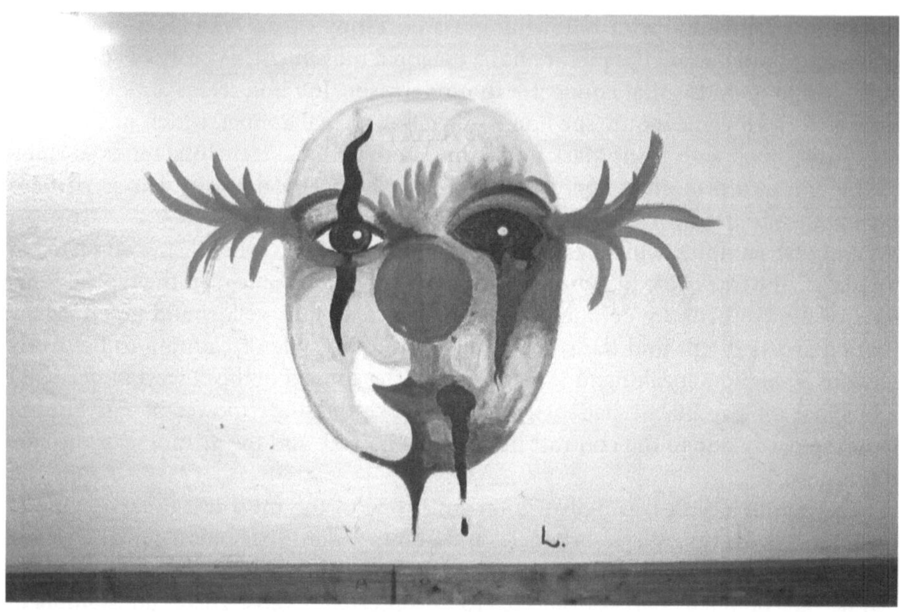

can Keith Haring. The artist has filled his or her entire allotted space with images, in keeping with the phenomenon of horror vacui, known from mediaeval art, in which the "fear of emptiness" meant that no part of a surface was left unadorned. Perhaps a modern parallel to this phenomenon is the adornment of walls in institutions such as prisons and hospitals (the culvert at Lillhagen Hospital is an example of this), as well as graffiti along tunnels and highways. To elaborate on the ideas of Prinzhorn, there seems to be an instinctive drive to create something where there is emptiness. The inclination to fill an entire space is also a recurring feature in outsider art. Wölfli, the patient studied by Morgenthaler, is an example of an artist who intricately adorned every part of his canvases. Since this compositional feature appears to be independent of the conscious creative intention of the artist, it can be connected to the fundamental creative instinct posited by Prinzhorn.

The landscape of freedom

This landscape is painted in idyllic clarity, in light colours. Its broad vistas suggest freedom and limitless possibilities, but perhaps also the risk of exposure to unknown hostile forces and loneliness. From a vertical crack in the mountain, a male figure peeks forth. Here is another reference to the source of life, the female body. Is the man in the mountain going through a kind of rebirth? Perhaps the situation of humanity in civilisation can be likened to being locked inside a mountain, waiting to be born again. Or do we see a metaphor for reaching outside oneself, a transition from the inner world to the outer reality? For patients in psychiatric care, the difference between life on the inside and in the outside can be monumental. The patient can feel small and insecure in the big world, beyond the security of the hospital.

In another large landscape that adorns an intersection in the culvert system, we see three trees against a starkly lit backdrop; the bright light is almost searing and painful. The artist has shaped the trees in a naturalistic manner but uses a more impressionist technique for most of the surrounding landscape, in mottled hues. The upper limit of the painting is unclear. It seems that there is an uncertainty as to where the image ends and reality begins. This is a question that is relevant for the psychiatric patient, and indeed for everyone: what is the difference between the image and reality? Or, metaphorically, what is part of the inner, psychic world, and what belongs to the exterior, material world? Where is the boundary between inner images and reality, and is it always clear? Or is it blurred sometimes? Does the inner world affect the outer world, and the other way around? In the idealisation of outsider art in the early 20th century, outsider artists were celebrated for giving primacy to their inner worlds, their private images, if you will, over objective reality. But might there also be a drawback, if the subjective imagery collides with the real world? The strong light in this landscape painting can be interpreted as illuminating a dark solitude, bringing painful but potentially constructive clarity.

What we see can be a matter of psychological perspective. In one of the more remarkable paintings in the culvert, painted on a board that has been attached to the wall, one sees either an expressionist landscape with a waterfall, the water becoming darker as it crashes down towards the viewer, or an abstracted woman in a billowing blue dress. Both visions of the painting are valid. Perhaps they can affect the viewer simultaneously, even if only one of the two images can be perceived consciously.

In another fresco we see a landscape built up of monochrome fields of colour, in bright, clear colours. The various elements in a mountainous terrain are melded together by the interplay of leaning shapes within the overall diagonal composition.

The work shows stylistic similarities with synthetism, a style that was championed by the French post-impressionist Paul Gauguin, among others, but updated in a more modernist idiom. The strong colours add to the landscape's modernist character.

The aquarium painting, too, is a kind of landscape, or rather seascape. While conventional and quite unsophisticated in style, the subject matter is vertiginous: an aquarium viewed from the inside, identifying us, the viewers, with the fishes in the aquarium. Is it a metaphor for the patients' existence, in which they are viewed, like alien creatures, from medical authorities on the outside, as if through the glass of an aquarium?

Dreams of beauty and vitality

Some of the paintings in the culvert possess a dream-like quality. In an urban scene, two high-rise buildings in clear blue and red stand out against a background in which shimmering yellow and green are intermixed. But the scene is not only dream-like due to its style and the artist's choice of colours. The street in front of the house is made up of a peacock's feathers. The peacock is a symbol of eternal life in early Christian art, and next to the high-rises, an enormous eye looks out over the cityscape. The all-seeing eye can represent an exterior power that critically examines the self. The evil eye, and different ways of protecting oneself against it, are features of many cultures.

Flowers are a motif in art with various connotations, but they are often linked to beauty, life, and mortality: the flower is beautiful and attracts insects that pollenate other flowers, but it is transient, it will soon wither and die. In the 1930s in Gothenburg, the Gothenburg colourist Ivan Ivarson used to receive unsold flowers from a florist at Kungstorget, which he loved to paint in bright colours. The American artist Georgia O'Keefe is famous for painting flowers in an extreme close-up, flowers that seem to become images of the body. The artist who paints these flowers in bright, swirling colours seems to relish both the energy of colour and the vital symbolism of the motif.

In a more conventional flower painting, in the genre of still life, a naïve mode of expression has been executed with touching care and precision. The painting does not encompass perspective, but this lack imbues it with a surreal charge, reminiscent of the works of the French artist Henri Rousseau, "Le Douanier" (the toll administrator), a self-taught painter who became an important figure in the Parisian avant-garde around 1900. Together with van Gogh and Cézanne, Rousseau inspired the breakthrough of modernism, which broke with the conventions of perspective and naturalism in art. In his art, like the art of the psychiatric patients discussed by Réja, Morgenthaler and Prinzhorn, technical deficiencies and force of expression are not mutually exclusive. On the contrary, the absence of technical finesse adds earnestness and a magical quality.

The Asylum of Art

This text has presented a background to the question of art and psychic suffering. The artworks in the culvert at Lillhagen Hospital, created by psychiatric patients in the late 1980s and early 1990s, are interpreted in the context of art history and the interest in the art of psychiatric patients that arose in the early 20th century, which was part of the breakthrough of modernism. At this time, the creative acts of psychiatric patients were evaluated and analysed as art, and were attributed specific qualities such as spontaneity, authenticity and freedom from conventions.

The unexpected discovery of these works, and the risk that they soon might be lost due to rebuilding, contribute to the way we perceive them in their context. They bear witness to an era in psychiatric care in Sweden, when art courses were available for patients in the setting of the total institution. They are also testament to the creativity of the individual patients, their will to express themselves and desire to leave a trace in their environment. Artistically, they can be considered ambitious amateur art, not lacking creative and moving elements, which are augmented by the interpretations possible in the specific context: namely the fact that they are works by institutionalised psychiatric patients, outcasts of society who in general have difficulties in making their voices heard. The artworks in the culvert are expressions of life, longing, love and the desire for freedom, created by individuals marked by isolation, limitations and disappointments. Did making art broaden their horizons and open new possibilities for them? Was their work, as in the creativity of Orpheus, connected to irreconcilable loss and a longing that knew no boundaries? Was art an area in their lives where they, in contrast to most other areas, could be free?

Clearly, the artists made efforts to achieve the best art they could. The supplement of meaning achieved simply by being able to work with something should not be underestimated, but the patients/artists also achieved creative success, in their way. Basic human drives to come to the fore in works that depict their themes in visual modes that are at times naïve and conventional, at times symbolic and mysterious, but always honest and direct. Through these works, a world stands out from the shadows of time. Another crucial function of art is the preservation of memory. The artworks in the culvert remind us of the dream reality of an institutional form of life, within the protected space of the asylum, that is perhaps gone forever.

Reflections

Inez Edström

In 2018, we launched the art studio at Östra Sjukhuset, where I work. The hospital art studio project began in 2017. The first studio was initiated by visual artist and psychiatric aide Stefan Karlsson and is situated as the Art studio at the Affective care unit, Sahlgrenska University hospital, Gothenburg, Sweden.[1] The studio is led by Karlsson, together with managers and staff members at Sahlgrenska. The aim is to support meaning making and a sense of connectedness among the patients.

For my part, I am at the art studio at Östra Sjukhuset twice a week, Mondays and Wednesdays. I usually arrive around lunchtime. Upon arrival, I begin by doing the rounds. I go through the four wards that are connected to the art studio and speak with healthcare personnel and patients to see who might be interested in taking part in art studio activities that day. I also make sure to inform potential new patients about the art studio program. The studio itself is open from 1pm until 7pm. We have an "open door" policy that allows participants to come and go as they please. The open door policy is an important aspect of the studio. A patient might have an appointment with a doctor, or they may have visitors. Perhaps someone is tired and wishes to sleep for a few hours, or they might be occupied with something else that day.

I like to have the art studio open in the afternoon, as well as in the evening, as there are often many planned activities happening during daytime hours, but there is usually very little going on in the wards during the evenings. This open door policy and range of studio hours makes it possible for patients to come and go as it best suits them. When I arrive at 1pm sharp with the coffee pot in hand, some patients are standing by the door waiting to enter, and some stay until closing. Other patients may drop by in the middle of the afternoon and stay for half an hour or so, and are just as happy with that. Energy and concentration are two resources that vary from one patient to another, and what one takes with you from the studio isn't connected to the length of time you spend there.

So what do we actually DO in the studio? Well, it differs a lot. I have a range of different materials to offer: from acrylic paint and watercolor, to the very best graphic art pens and pencils, to modeling clay for sculptures. We have a large range of papers, brushes, pens, etc. It is important that the studio and supplies feel gener-

1 https://konstateljen.org/om/

ous and convenient. I hope to facilitate an environment that makes it feel easy to start creating. This is also why I do not clean up too much. If there is paint everywhere and everything is out on the table, one is less likely to be intimidated or afraid of making a mess. I find it more conducive for participants to be able to easily reach for any art supply that sparks their interest and just start creating. We also have a small art library, as well as the internet for inspiration. I always keep an open ear to listen for what we may be able to improve in terms of materials. If someone has a specific technique or material with which they like to work, it is possible that others will like it, too, so I often see if it is something I am able acquire for the studio.

Another important aspect of the time spent in the art studio is that it is best if the activity in itself is not set or planned. I don't say, "Today we're going to learn to paint watercolor landscapes." Everyone is able to do what they wish, when they wish, and if all the different possibilities and choices feel overwhelming (which they sometimes do), we figure something out together – you and I, together.

The level of experience varies among participants. But that doesn't really matter. Everyone has their own reasons for being there. For some, it is about rediscovering an activity they have forgotten about or that they have felt they cannot do when they are ill. Some patients have not drawn or painted since elementary school, or ever for that matter, and the studio becomes a step towards drawing or painting as an adult, hopefully without putting too much pressure on themselves. Some of the patients are already painters, either on a professional level or as a hobby. In those cases, I might not be able to offer much in the way of teaching or technical advice, but I am able to provide the materials and a space for them to continue working on their painting during their time as inpatients. Some patients come to the studio and really want to learn a specific technique: "Could you teach me how to paint with watercolor?" or "Can you teach me how to draw perspective?" Then that is where we place our focus.

We are a very diverse group. Participants have been admitted to the hospital for a variety of reasons. Some may be diagnosed with bipolar disorder or depression, have anxiety or have been feeling suicidal, while others may be in the midst of a crisis in their lives. The ages of participants may range from 18 to 70 years old. For some, it is their first time as an inpatient in a psychiatric ward; for others it is their thirty-first. When engaging in activities at the art studio, all of these different parameters come into play. If someone is in a state of hypomania, for example, they may experience difficulty concentrating and engaging in meticulous, precise work. We may then need to find a fast and effective method of creating art that is better suited to their needs at that time. For some it is the complete opposite, maybe someone needs an escape or distraction from dark thoughts or from anxiety and really needs or wants to dive into that kind of meticulous, detailed work. Like the mandala, often used as a mindfulness tool, creating detailed and complex drawings, or clay sculptures, may offer an escape from thoughts of anxiety and distress. Sometimes people come just to hang out, talk, socialize and have some coffee. Perhaps after a while, they may begin creating something, perhaps not. Either way is fine by me. It's all welcome.

An important part of the art studio time is the social aspect and conversation. Sometimes people share their thoughts and feelings regarding their current situations, or discuss how they are feeling right now at the moment as they are creating. Sometimes they speak about everything else in life other than their diagnosis or treatment: interpersonal relationships, current affairs, a new song from a favorite artist, what their favorite breakfast was as a child. We all exchange experiences, thoughts and stories – the patients, the healthcare personnel and me. Something freeing happens in the conversation when your hands are occupied at the same time, reminiscent of play therapies. It becomes a less demanding conversation. A while ago one patient told me, "Thank you for the conversation we had in the studio last week. For a couple of hours I didn't feel like a patient, but just like a regular person talking to other adults. That was so important for me." Since I am not an official staff member involved in their healthcare, but rather a semi-outsider, the patients are sometimes able to feel relaxed in a different way with me than with the healthcare personnel. Different rules apply. I do not read their charts. The contents of our conversations are not written down and filed. I do not know anything about their backgrounds, only what they have told me. It is completely up to each individual how much they wish to share. I can be a support if that is what they wish for me to be, but I can also just be an art teacher, who provides technical instruction about how to paint, if that is what you wish. I want participants to feel in control of the social situation. It is completely up to each individual how open they wish to be with me, and how they wish to use their time in the art studio.

The healthcare personnel at the hospital play an important role in motivating the patients. For no matter how wonderful the art studio is, if a patient is feeling tormented by anxiety or overwhelmed with depression, it may be very difficult for someone to try something new, or to even just leave their room. In those instances, sometimes the healthcare personnel may be able to provide support and encouragement when providing information about the art studio. With that said, I've found that the very best advertisers are the patients themselves. Nothing seems to beat when one patient at the ward has discovered the studio and in their excitement tells the others to join. When that happens, the studio gets really busy!

When I began working at the art studio many people asked me about my work there. They seemed to have the assumption that the artwork produced by persons at an inpatient psychiatric hospital was likely to be difficult or dark. Admittedly, in the beginning it was a worry of mine as well, but this worry was highly overrated. I've found that more often people paint their goals and visions, rather than the potential darkness they might be experiencing at the moment. Perhaps when one is involuntarily surrounded by a lot of darkness, one feels no need to add to that, but rather work with creating a contrast to that darkness. Or perhaps the artwork is a way of working with or through that darkness. With that said, I do not pass judgment or have rules about what is right or wrong in terms of the work created, or one's motives for creating. Art is about the process of creating the artwork itself. When we talk, we may talk about the paintings, drawings and sculptures created, the technique used, or the process of creating. I am not an art therapist and it is not my job to analyze. My job is to help art studio participants create artwork, to help them find strength and hopefully some joy in the creative process. We are not engaging in art therapy, per se. We are creating art. Though I do believe creating art in the studio surely can have therapeutic benefits. We work on not criticizing ourselves in the studio, which sometimes can be difficult. I prefer to focus on finding the strengths inherent in all the works created and to be constructive, rather than criticize or critique. In the art studio, I hope to give everyone a sense of "I can."

The art activities at Lillhagen and their relevance for current psychiatry

Elizabeth Punzi

Psychiatry is a discipline that involves a variety of perspectives, bio-medically as well as socially-oriented. During the last decades of the 20th century, bio-medical perspectives became hegemonic, and during the same period psychiatry went through varying social reform processes. During these processes, the psychiatric institutions were questioned and subsequently deconstructed, and the re-socializing of "patients"[1] into the civil society was in focus (Haack & Kumbier, 2012). These transformations have been named de-hospitalization, trans-institutionalization, and de-institutionalization (Topor, Andersson, Bülow, Stefansson, & Denhov, 2016). I use the term de-institutionalization since it refers to the dismantling of the large institutions and the considerable reduction in the number of hospital beds. This term de-institutionalization has however been criticized, since institutions are more than buildings and the number of beds. The de-institutionalization was also driven by liberation movements. Survivors of psychiatry witnessed abuse and protested against inequality, institutionalization, and oppression, and critical health professionals and stakeholders strived for social and psychotherapeutic perspectives (Crafoord, 1987; Dwyer, 2018; Morrow, 2007; Starkman, 2013). In Sweden, the "Reform of psychiatry" was implemented in 1995 (Socialstyrelsen, 1999). The reform meant that individuals with various forms of psychosocial distress should not be treated in institutions. Instead psychiatric care, living conditions, and daily activities should be integrated in the civil society. The results of the reform are not straightforward. Some individuals came to live under precarious circumstances and experienced new forms of oppression, whereas others do well and live satisfying lives with minimal contacts with psychiatry or social services.

The reform processes in the last decades of the 20th century were influenced by social psychiatry with its focus on non-physician-centered perspectives, re-socialization of the "patients," as well as a striving to develop alternative non-medical in-

1 There are many terms that describe individuals who seek out, or are forced to receive, psychiatric care. Here the word "patient", in quotations marks is used, in line with Burstow's (2013) recommendation. The word "patient" describes the position of the patient and simultaneously acknowledges that medical and governmental term needs to be problematized since such words might cover up questions of social context or meaning making.

terventions, for example leisure activities, including art activities (Haack & Kumbier, 2012). From this perspective, art is seen as part of human life and expression, and "patients," once again just like anyone, might sense that art provides meaning, joy, and opportunities for self-expression. There are undoubtedly "patients" who are talented and skillful artists but the focus of arts in psychiatry is foremost on the creative process and the opportunities this process holds (McNiff, 1998). It should also be noted that art might be a medium for criticism and resistance toward historical as well as current oppression.

Current mainstream psychiatry is, however, focused on quantification, standardization, and documentation that provide "evidence" of what has been "produced," "an approach that is related to the idea that human care organisations should be managed according to incentives in the business sector (Harris, 2014; Forsell & Ivarsson Westberg, 2014; Montalto, 2014) leaving limited room for expressive activities centered on meaning, joy, criticism, or self-expression. Despite, or because of this, there is an increased and renewed interest in the importance of the arts for recovery (Stickley & Hui, 2012). Studies that investigate art activities often concern activities that take place outside hospitals. This is relevant since the main part of the in-patient units have been dismantled, and art activities are accordingly predominantly connected to out-patient units; often realized by social service units and/or activity centers for users of psychiatry. Despite the reforms and deconstructions of the major part of the old institutions, there are, however, still in-patient units, and since "patients" might be there for several weeks or even months, stakeholders want to offer meaningful activities (De Vecchi, Kenny, & Kidd, 2015). "Patients" themselves tend to underline that art is central to meaning making, belonging, positive identity, and self-confidence (Van Lith, 2014) and that relationships are fundamental for recovery (Banerjee & Basu, 2014; Topor, Böe, & Larsen, 2018). Art activities indeed involve relational interaction between the participants, as well as between participants and those who lead the activities. These relations contribute to experiences of self-confidence, support, belonging, and positive identity (De Vecchi et al., 2015).

Current strivings to integrate art activities could beneficially be informed by art activities in the history of psychiatry, such as the ones at Lillhagen. Thoughtful remembrance of psychiatry and its heritage in the form of buildings, practices, and artwork created by "patients" is important for understanding the prerequisites of psychiatric treatment, throughout history and today. It should be noted that former institutions were oppressive and abusive (Dwyer, 2018; Reaume, 1994). There were however also examples of humane approaches and activities, including opportunities to engage in art (Hogan, 2011; Svedberg, 2014). It should also be noted that art activities could be implemented and realized by non-medically trained professionals and artists (Hogan, 2001; White, 1989). This approach resonates with social psychiatry's strivings to establish non-medical interventions.

I submit that if humane approaches in the history of psychiatry are acknowledged, there are increased possibilities to establish humane approaches and activities that enhance supportive relationships and meaning making in current psychiatry. Accordingly, I try to gain knowledge about how art activities were performed at

Lillhagen, and try to understand the interactions that surrounded them. I therefore performed interviews with non-medical employees who worked at Lillhagen from the 1960s until the 1990s, studied brochures about the art activities, and reflected on the murals made by "patients." I wanted to listen to those who were not medically trained.[2]

Lillhagen hospital was located outside Gothenburg, Sweden's second largest town with about 500,000 inhabitants. In the 1970s there was room for about 2000 "patients." From the last decades of the 20th century until the beginning of the 21st century, Lillhagen was dismantled. As recently as 2018, buildings were demolished. Some buildings have been reshaped, and considerable parts of the hospital are being transformed into a residential area.

In the 1950s, artist Bengt Dimming initiated painting courses for "patients." During the 1960s, more courses were established. In Sweden, there are organizations that provide adult education in the form of courses that often concern arts, foreign languages, literature, music, or handicraft. Those organizations are named studieförbund (educational associations). They were established in the beginning of the 20th century and receive funding from the Swedish state. One such educational association was in charge of the courses at Lillhagen. During the 1960s and the 1970s there were courses in, for example, visual arts, sculpture, and literature, as well as weekly lectures about art and literature, and drama groups. Visits to art exhibitions, concerts, and museums were also arranged. From the late 1960s, Lillhagen became specifically known for its' many art activities. The artworks were exhibited at private galleries, community centers, and at the City art gallery of Gothenburg. "Patients" also created murals in Lillhagen's basement. About 30 murals still decorate the walls of the basement that today is used for transportation between residential homes and rehabilitation centers in the area.

Some of those I interviewed had worked at Lillhagen in the late 1960s, others started working there in the 1970s. Two were visual artists (henceforth named artists). One of them identified as a painter, the other as a textile artist. The third person was a writer. These three worked directly with the art activities; two were employed by the educational association, one was employed by the hospital. The fourth person I spoke to was an untrained psychiatric aide who was employed by the educational association and worked at the hospital library assisting "patients" when they borrowed books, instruments, or records. Finally, I spoke to two custodians, mainly working with transportation, maintenance, and repairs. They had interacted with the "patients" on a daily basis when "patients" moved around in the hospital area, for example to and from activities and when the basements were painted. In order to protect the privacy of those I spoke to, further details are not presented.

I asked those I interviewed to describe when s/he worked at Lillhagen, what kind of duties s/he had, the spaces s/he had worked in, and how the work was organized. I also asked them to describe their memories of the art activities and the other leisure activities, and how they perceived the interaction with the "patients."

2 It should be acknowledged that creative activities also were established by medically trained professionals, not least occupational therapist. This paper however concerns art activities that were framed as non-medical interventions.

During the 1970s, brochures that presented the courses and activities arranged by the educational association were administered to the "patients." Other brochures were administered during exhibitions. One interviewee gave me a bunch of brochures that presented courses and exhibitions. These brochures illustrate the "atmosphere" of the art activities, the approach toward the "patients" and how the artwork was presented.

The walls of the basement were originally decorated in red and yellow; red signified that the area was connected to the section for women and yellow signified the section for men (Stadsfullmäktiges i Göteborg byggnadskommitté, 1935). The first murals were painted in the 1970s and the last ones in the early 1990s. They are part of a material heritage that provides insight about psychiatry during this era.

It is important to acknowledge that I did not interview any "patients" Thereby, there is a risk that "patients" perspectives are forgotten and also that the "patients" become objectified. It should therefore be noted that none of the interviewees expressed distancing tendencies toward the "patients." On the contrary they spoke in non-pathologizing, and empathic ways. I have strived to capture this in the tone of the text.

As a practitioner and a clinical researcher, my own experiences and perspectives inevitably influence this text. As a practitioner, I have worked with "patients" with considerable psychosocial distress, and I am skeptical about, or openly critical toward, the current focus on diagnostic entities, structured interventions, and insistence on symptom reduction as the major treatment aim. I work and write from humanistic and critical perspectives and tend to focus on social context, meaning making, and processes of recovery (Davidson, 2016; Deegan, 2002). I have a specific interest in creative activities and the heritage of psychiatry. My pre-understanding

might create a biased approach as well as a false, or at least superficial, sense of understanding, and I might have failed to ask exploring questions to those I interviewed. I have tried to counteract this through asking for concrete examples and personal memories. Moreover, a colleague with clinical experience and knowledge about social psychiatry and recovery oriented practice, who is involved in research concerning the history of psychiatry, read the text and made suggestions on how it could be improved. Changes were made according to their suggestions.

The interviews, the brochures and the reflections on the murals:

Flexibility

The art activities at Lillhagen were framed as courses that lasted for a semester and "patients" were invited to participate. The courses were free of charge and those who were interested were welcome to contact the course leaders directly. A variety of courses were offered; often concerning art activities, but also cooking, Swedish for migrants, foreign languages, and typewriting. The brochures give an impression of curiosity and openness. In line with this impression, the interviewees described possibilities to adapt activities to the needs of the participants and also related that the activities were flexibly developed according to ideas presented by the participants. If the participants, for example, had ideas about art techniques they wanted to learn or certain artists they wanted to know more about, it was possible to adapt the courses to their wishes, arrange a lecture, or start a new activity.

The interviewee who worked at the library also described a sense of flexibility and openness. If the "patient" and the staff member, for example, had a shared interest in some specific form of music, art, or literature, it was possible to leave the desk, take a walk and discuss the common interest. The "patients" were encouraged to suggest books or records that could be purchased and staff members from the library sometimes worked with the leaders of the activities and, for example, assisted the artist and the "patients."

The descriptions of flexibility and openness were not attempts to whitewash the past. The interviewees spoke about oppression and derogatory views of the "patients" but sensed that alongside this, there were humane practices and approaches that should be remembered. The artists and the writer described that the participant's diagnosis never was central during the art activities. They approached the "patients" as course participants and adapted instructions and activities to their needs, interests, and capacities, just as in any education they had been involved in. The artists also strived to adapt the activities to the situation. One interviewee, for example, described that one day when the first snow fell, some participants approached the leaders and said that they wanted to go outside to make snow sculptures. The artists, the participants and some staff members went outside, made snow sculptures, played in the snow, and some of them threw snowballs.

The artists who had been employed by the hospital had worked at in-patient wards for "patients" with drug addiction. The reason for this arrangement was that the "patients" at these wards were not permitted to leave the wards, and the staff members and the head psychiatrist at the wards sensed that "their patients" also should have the possibility to engage in art.

Approaching without disturbing

Throughout the interviews, it came forth that everyone had strived to approach and support each "patient" as a unique person. When the interviewees spoke about the interaction between themselves, medical as well as non-medical staff members, and "patients," it also came forth that the art activities were not an exclusive concern for the artists. Medical staff members and psychiatric aides could visit the studios. It was however mutually agreed that the participants should not be disturbed. Moreover, during coffee breaks, clients, artists and other staff members sat together for a Swedish "fika." It should be noted that "fika" is more than a coffee break; it signifies a social meeting that means to sit down together, socialize, chat, and have coffee and cookies.

The two custodians also described strivings to carry out their tasks without disturbing the "patients." They remembered how "patients" could prefer to walk certain routes or rest in certain places in the hospital area, and how they and the other custodians adapted their tasks to the routines of the "patients." They, for example, changed transportation routes in the basement so that "patients" did not have to change their routes.

The murals are the only remnants of the art activities and of the former "patients," depicting landscapes, mythological themes, and/or people. A few present uncanny motifs. Others present humoristic motifs. The custodians remembered the painting of the murals as a period characterized by intense work as well as by joy and liveliness. "The basement was so alive, and the atmosphere was great. You should have seen it!" one of them said. Some "patients" had discussed their work with the custodians who sensed that some "patients" seemed to enjoy opportunities to talk and get to know the employees. Others concentrated on their work and did not want to be disturbed, and could be angry or frustrated if they were interrupted.

The artists underlined that they did not want to impose their own ideas on the participants but rather strived to respect their work and their need to concentrate and find their own expression and style. They underlined that the "patients" were course participants. Accordingly, they strived to support them to develop skills and the capacity to master varying techniques so that they could realize their artworks.

The dismantling of Lillhagen

From the 1980s, when Lillhagen was continuously dismantled, the art activities were downsized and transferred to facilities in varying parts of Gothenburg. One interviewee described that this change had a negative effect on "the soul of the activities." The activities became located in institutions that were not perceived as negative in themselves but since both the leader of the activities and the participants were "visitors" in these institutions, it was difficult to create a holding environment, continuity, and a sense of togetherness. The leaders of the activities had to transport themselves and the equipment all over town. Altogether this created a sense of "homelessness." It was also stressful. Accordingly, several leaders resigned and were not replaced.

Before the dismantling of Lillhagen, murals, as well as paintings on canvases, decorated the basements. When Lillhagen was dismantled some paintings were saved, others were stolen, some were transferred to retirement homes to decorate the walls there, and some were thrown away. The interviewees questioned how this could have happened and sensed that more efforts should have been made to save the artworks. Some also asked whether it was permitted to throw so many paintings away or to let them be destroyed. Who did they belong to? Did not "patients" have the rights to their own artwork?

Rumors say that a considerable number of "patients" returned to stay in the basement when Lillhagen was dismantled. According to the custodians, there were some former "patients" who directly after the dismantling returned to Lillhagen. Since the custodians knew them, they tried to support them and could invite them for a "fika." Some former "patients" had spent some nights in the basement. Those were few, however, and the custodians sensed that the rumors were exaggerated.

The people I interviewed did not idealize Lillhagen. On the contrary, they described many aspects of the institutions as degrading. Some buildings were in a state of serious decline, facilities could be dirty, the hospitalization of "patients" inhumane, and they described that "patients" could be badly treated. Moreover, some interviewees wondered about the diagnoses and assessments of the "patients." After the de-institutionalization, they could meet former course participants who worked and seemed to live satisfying lives even though they had been labeled as incurable. The interviewees asked themselves, and me, whether these individuals had been ap-

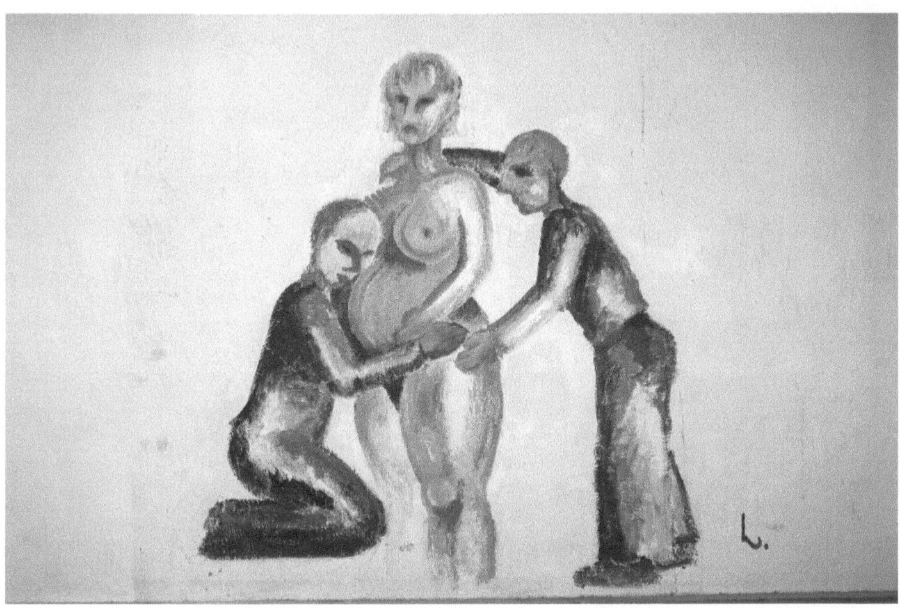

propriately understood and treated. Nevertheless, they sensed that the positive aspects of Lillhagen should also be remembered.

Some interviewees related that after the de-institutionalization, they had known where some former course participants worked and sometimes went to see them to have a chat. One interviewee described that a former participant once said; "Do you remember how much fun we had?" when they spoke about the art activities. This comment gave the interviewee a sense that the art activities had been meaningful on a long-standing level, and that the artists, staff members, and the participants had created something meaningful together.

Reflections

The people I spoke to sensed that the art courses at Lillhagen were characterized by openness, flexibility, and strivings to support "patients" without disturbing them. The course leaders could initiate and develop activities together with the participants and the psychiatric aide, and the custodians could change routines when they considered it important for the "patients." It was, however, difficult to continue the activities during the de-institutionalization. The atmosphere was lost.

In current mainstream psychiatry, classification, structured interventions, and symptom reduction are often in focus, and accordingly, contextual factors and acknowledgement of human diversity run the risk of being underestimated or excluded (Lewis, 2009; Moncrieff 2014; Timimi 2011). Despite, or because of this, there is simultaneously an increased focus on person-centered care and the importance of meaning making and belonging (Davidson, 2016; Duff, Rubenstein, & Prilleltensky, 2016). The person-centered and non-governing approach to art activities that came

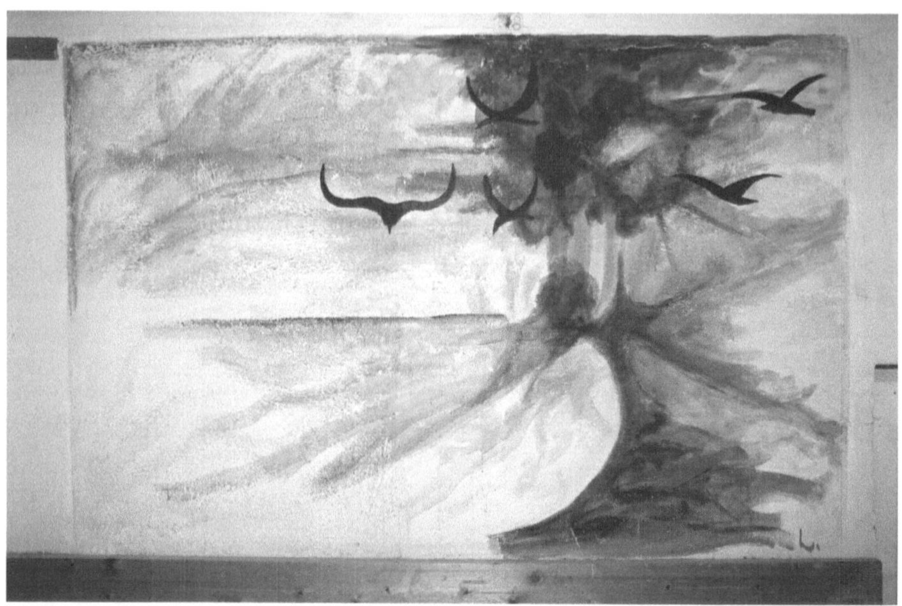

forth in this study, is thus in line with current recovery-oriented perspectives and strivings to provide individual treatment that acknowledges compassion, personal preferences, agency, and contextual factors (Banerjee & Basu, 2014; Larson & Topor, 2017; Macbeth & Gumley, 2012).

Moreover, the strivings to approach "patients" without disturbing them are in line with many current art activities that are arranged as courses or programs and aim at an active life, sense of belonging, and positive identity among the participants. Such activities are often arranged outside psychiatric institutions and hospitals. Since in-patient treatment seldom is performed for longer periods, long-term activities in the form of courses or programs are difficult to establish within current psychiatric hospitals. I would, however, like to suggest that art activities at in-patient units are possible, as well as needed, in order to support meaning making, agency, and self-expressions. Art activities have been flexibly integrated in psychiatry in earlier times and so they could be today. Given the short hospital stays, it is difficult to establish longer courses or engage in long-term decorations of basement or other spaces. Nevertheless, "patients" could be invited to engage with art in less structured ways. Art studios could be open to "patients" regardless of whether they have the opportunity to engage with painting on one or several occasions. There are indeed current pilot projects in Swedish inpatient psychiatry that are centered on inviting in-patients to flexible artistic activities centered on, for example, visual art or creative writing. Also those who participate one or two times could perceive the activities as meaningful and the experience of painting could support new perceptions of oneself or inspire self expression. Art studios could be run by artists, or writers, who support and instruct the participants in their creative expression regardless of the length of the hospital stays. Such a non-governing approach could be a positive experience for "patients" who often are used to being assessed, classified, and even constrained and coerced. It should, however, be noted that in a climate centered on classification and symptom reduction, art activities might become instrumental, used to support health in structured ways. Such approaches underestimate the importance of flexibility and the creative process and thereby might defuse the opportunities to promote well-being and self-expression (McNiff, 1998). Current psychiatry could beneficially be inspired by prior art activities that were open and flexible and emphasized the unique person rather than diagnoses and structured methods. The flexibility and openness also concerned spaces and interiors. The "patients" could create spaces for themselves and they could also leave visible traces in the form of artwork, an approach that could inspire current psychiatry.

The murals are traces of individuals who in some cases lived major parts of their lives at Lillhagen and other institutions. In the process of de-institutionalization, their narratives became excluded. It is ethically necessary to reflect on how the "patients," their experiences, narratives, and artwork could be remembered and honored. This does not mean that their artwork should be exhibited at museums. Remembrance needs to be performed with thoughtfulness and in collaboration with "patients" otherwise they might contribute to marginalization and/or sensationalism (MacKinnon & Coleborne, 2013; Rodéhn, 2019). It should be noted that some former "patients" sense that the institutions should be demolished and forgotten, while others sense that there should be places of remembrance and accordingly want to influence how remnants are handled and presented. It should also be acknowledged that some "patients," just like the people I spoke to, sensed that the old institutions paradoxically could contribute to a sense of belonging that was lost in the de-institutionalization (Shimrat, 2013). Accordingly, there are no straightforward answers to the questions of how the heritage of psychiatry should be handled. Every decision needs to be reflected upon.

The history of psychiatry is shameful, with examples of abuse and oppression that are beyond the imaginable (Dwyer, 2018; Reaume, 1994). At the same time, the dark history of psychiatry might take attention from that fact that current practices might be equally oppressive. Humane approaches in the history of psychiatry, as well as remembrance of artists, art educators, and staff members who advocated for patients' rights and dignity, should be remembered since they show that alternatives are possible. Moreover, they show us that we might learn from the past.

References

- Banerjee, P., & Basu, J. (2014). Therapeutic relationship as a change agent in psychotherapy: An interpretative phenomenological analysis. *Journal of Humanistic Psychology*, 56, 171-193.
- Burstow, B. (2013). A rose by any other name. In B.A. LeFrancois, R. Menzies and G. Reaume (Eds.), *Mad matters. A critical reader in Canadian Mad studies* (pp. 79-90). Toronto: Canadian Scholars' Press.

– Crafoord, C. (1987). *Den möjliga och omöjliga psykiatrin.* [The possible and impossible psychiatry]. Stockholm: Natur & Kultur.
– Davidson, L. (2016). The recovery movement: Implications for mental health care and enabling people to participate fully in life. *Health Affairs*, 35, 1091-1097.
– De Vecchi, N., Kenny, A., & Kidd, S. (2015). Stakeholder views in a recovery-oriented psychiatric rehabilitation art therapy program in a rural Australian mental health service: a qualitative description. *International Journal of Mental Health Systems*, 9, 1-11.
– Deegan, P.E. (2002). Recovery as a self-directed process of healing and transformation. *Occupational Therapy in Mental Health*, 17, 5-21.
– Duff, J., Rubenstein, C., & Prilleltensky, I. (2016). Wellness and fairness: Two core values for humanistic psychology. *The Humanistic Psychologist*, 44, 127-141.
– Dwyer, E. (2018). The final years of Central State Hospital. *Journal of the History of Medicine and Allied Science,* 74, 107-126.
– Forsell, A., & Ivarsson Westberg, A. (2014). *Administrationssamhället.* [The administration society]. Lund: Studentlitteratur.
– Haack, K., & Kumbier, E. (2012). History of social psychiatry. *Current Opinion in Psychiatry*, 25, 492-496.
– Hogan S. (2001). *Healing arts. The history of art therapy*, London: Jessica Kingsley.
– Lewis, B. (2009). *Moving beyond Prozac, DSM, and the new psychiatry. The birth of postpsychiatry.* Ann Arbor: The University of Michigan Press.
– Macbeth, A., & Gumley, A. (2012). Exploring compassion: A meta-analysis of the association between self-compassion and psychopathology. *Clinical Psychology Review*, 32, 545-552.
– MacKinnon, D., & Coleborne, C. (2013). Seeing and not seeing psychiatry. In C. Coleborne and D. MacKinnon (Eds.) *Exhibiting madness in museums. Remembering psychiatry through collections and display*, (pp. 3-13). New York: Routledge.
– McNiff, S. (1998). *Trust the process. An artist's guide to letting go.* Boston: Shambhala.
– Mills, C. (2013). *Decolonizing global mental health. The psychiatrization of the majority world.* London: Routledge.
– Moncrieff, J. (2014). The medicalisation of "ups and downs": The marketing of the new bipolar disorder. *Transcultural Psychiatry*, 51, 581-598.
– Montalto, M. (2014). The ethical implications of using technology in psychological testing and treatment. *Ethical Human Psychology and Psychiatry*, 16, 127-136.
– Morrow, M. (2007). Critiquing the "psychiatric paradigm" revisited: Reflections on feminist interventions in mental health. *Resources for Feminist Research*, 32, 69-85.
– Reaume, G. (1994). Keep your labels off my mind! Or "Now I am going to pretend I am craze but don't be a bit alarmed": Psychiatric history from the patients' perspectives. *Canadian Bulletin of Medical History*, 11, 397-424.
– Rodéhn, C. (2019). Emotions in the museum of medicine. An investigation of how museum educators employ emotions and what these emotions do. International Journal of Heritage Studies. Published online ahead of print. *doi: 10.1080/13527258.2018.1557236*

- Shimrat, I. (2013). The tragic farce of "Community mental health care". In B.A. LeFrancois, R. Menzies and G. Reaume (Eds.), *Mad matters. A critical reader in Canadian Mad studies* (pp. 144-157). Toronto: Canadian Scholars' Press.
- Socialstyrelsen. (1999). *Välfärd och valfrihet? – Slutrapport från utvärderingen av 1995 års psykiatrireform.* [Welfare and freedom of choice? – Final report from the evaluation of the reform of psychiatry, 1995]. Stockholm: Socialstyrelsen.
- Stadsfullmäktiges i Göteborg byggnadskommitté. (1935). *Lillhagens sjukhus vid Göteborg.* [Lillhagen hospital Gothenburg]. Göteborg: Stadsfullmäktige.
- Starkman, M. (2013). The movement. In B.A. LeFrancois, R. Menzies and G. Reaume (Eds.), *Mad matters. A critical reader in Canadian Mad studies* (pp. 27-37). Toronto: Canadian Scholars' Press.
- Stickley, T., & Hui, A. (2012). Arts in-reach: taking 'bricks off shoulders' in adult mental health inpatient care. *Journal of Psychiatric and Mental Health Nursing*, 19, 402-409.
- Svedberg, G. (2014). *Hugo Lindblads förlorade drömmar – om en patient i vetenskapens tjänst.* [Hugo Lindblad's lost dreams – a client in the service of science]. Stockholm: Ersta Sköndal.
- Timimi, S. (2011). Globalising mental health: a neo-liberal project. *Ethnicity and Inequalities in Health and Social Care,* 4, 155-160.
- Topor, A., Andersson, G., Bülow, P., Stefansson, C-G., & Denhov. A. (2016). After the asylum? The new institutional landscape. *Community Mental Health Journal*, 56, 731-737.
- Topor, A., Böe, T.D., & Larsen, I.B. (2018). Small things, micro-affirmations and helpful professionals. Everyday recovery-oriented practices according to persons with mental health problems. *Community Mental Health Journal*, 54, 1212-1220.
- Van Lith, T. (2014). "Painting to find my spirit": Art making as the vehicle to find meaning and connection in the mental health recovery process. *Journal of Spirituality in Mental Health*, 16, 19-36.
- Vrotsou, K., Andersson, G., Ellegård, K., Stefansson, C-G., Topor, A., Denhov, A., & Bülow, P. (2017). A time-geographic approach for visualizing the paths of intervention for persons with severe mental illness. *Geografiska Annaler: Series B, Human Geography*, 99, 341-359.

The interlinked fluidity of art and mental health

Christian Munthe

When people identify some suffering or dysfunction, they place the problem within or outside of the person afflicted, and when they do the former, they view the problem as one of "health." Already in the case of somatic phenomena, to distinguish between the pathological and the normal can meet with well-known challenges of variability. While having the skin opened up by a sharp object is in some cases viewed as a potentially serious injury and health threat, in other social contexts it is viewed as a desirable, even necessary, act of social identity or ritual. In the one case, the same physical phenomenon may be appreciated as a sign of severe dysfunction, and in the other as one of normality. A generic example is how we view death and life-expectancy across history. Today, in the Western setting I'm writing from within, to die at the age of 70 is a tragedy, as the average life expectancy is around 85. However, hundred and fifty years before now, the same age would have been considered exceptional, as the average life at that time ended around 40.

This fluidity of what we consider (un)healthy is found also in the area of mental health, but now with a further twist. Here, we brand as disease or ill-health not only what makes life difficult and unfortunate for oneself. At least as important is how a person's psychology relates to others and to society: the dysfunctionality making something into a mental health problem is not seldom an inability to abide by social expectations and norms. Of course, this inability will often lead to harm for the person suffering the problem, through social exclusion and discrimination, but that harm will then be incidental and not part of what defines the health problem. A famous example is how homosexuality was a disease up to the beginning of the 1970s (or 1979 in Sweden), but then taken off the pathology list – not due to any new knowledge in psychiatry or biomedicine, but due to a moral shift on what romantic and sexual behaviors may be acceptable in society. Another example is the way that difficulties in dealing emotionally with life's hardships has moved the other direction – from normality to pathology – as norms regarding what we should be prepared to endure have changed in a socioeconomically changing society. What was before seen as an unfortunate but understandable emotional overload due to life's troubles and demands, has passed into the taxonomy of clinical depression and related disorders, thus signaling that the person is not responding as she should. Likewise, with a host of other diagnoses, labelling people ill who before may have been viewed as merely odd or difficult.

This has important consequences for a person suffering from a mental health problem. While a somatically ill or injured person will typically be viewed with unconditional compassion, a mentally ill person will always be seen, at least partly, as a threat and a deviant; as someone who breeches accepted norms regarding human behavior. Society and others may, of course, pity this person, but a main response has always been one of protection against the perceived danger through exclusion from society, and still is. Medicalization has to some extent offered remedy in this respect: temporarily facilitating some normality that allows the person to partially and temporarily re-enter society. But the condition for this inclusion is still set, not by the person herself, but by the views of others. This constitutes a well-known hurdle for effective management of mental health problems, with the risk of weak adherence to treatments due to side-effects, and resulting institutionalization or permanent exclusion, as well-known challenges that threaten to prolong the suffering of the afflicted person. This, in all, makes for a particularly difficult situation for a person burdened by mental ill-health to travel the rather long (sometimes lifelong) pathway towards (partial) improvement.

But norms may change to provide emancipation that allows the person to remain in his or her condition without social exclusion or harm, as the example of homosexuality illustrates. Moreover, existing social norms may allow protected spaces for controlled norm breaches, and such spaces may facilitate normative change. Sports is a well-known case: showing us (since long) how fierce physical competition need not include killing and maiming each other. I want to suggest that creative art is another such space – if not by definition, so by justification – and, in addition, a space that suits the predicament of those deemed mentally ill.

In the context of art it is not only allowed, but prescribed, to test and transgress the boundaries of ordinary experience and received opinion, and to explore, process and express that which otherwise would be judged unreal, disgusting, unfitting or immoral. This is one of the reasons why healthy people value art: it allows them (us?) to view and simulate what they (we?) fear the most – such as death, such as loss, such as chaos, such as madness. But art is not primarily about consumption. Creation of artistic works is the core of art – the fact that these works may then be enjoyed by others is a side-effect. And it is here – within artistic creativity – that we find the space for mentally ill persons to explore what meaning may be found in their conditions and hardships, and thereby to exist as they are without harmful exclusion, while waiting for ways to heal. In addition, within this space the very notion of what healing might be can be explored to facilitate a bearable pathway to face otherwise grim prospects of constraining conditions (unwanted medication, forsaken socioeconomic opportunities and restricted social relationships) that may have to be endured in order to re-enter society.

But the same art, thus created for emancipation and healing within the constraints of mental illness, may also help transform the social view of mental health that creates the aforementioned constraints. Norms may change, and the artistic creativity of mentally ill people may thus not only serve to empower themselves, but to transform socially embraced views of mental illness in a more emancipating direction. That very madness of art which makes it into what it is may serve to liberate both madness itself and the mad from harmful exclusion.

Hugo Lindblad: The Odd One In

Carl Abrahamsson

Where most creative inpatients face the dilemma of double anonymity (1. not being acknowledged by the outside, and 2. specifically not for their creativity), there are occasional exceptions that transcend or transgress the walls of psychiatric clinics and hospitals. These could even prove to be of assistance to further scientific progress and insight, if given the opportunity to express and explain themselves in their own words and/or art.

In 1919, Swedish designer and lithographer Hugo Lindblad (1885-1976) was admitted to Stockholms Hospital (a.k.a. Konradsberg), and diagnosed as a schizophrenic. This became one of many stays in various institutions for him. It was, however, clear to his doctors that he was out of the ordinary as far as schizophrenics go. Not only did he experience a great deal of fascinating things in his inner life; he also gladly communicated this in elaborate and stylish drawings and eloquent writing (in English as well as Swedish). Despite the fact that he couldn't properly handle the general demands of the outside world, he seems to have been blessed with the ability to communicate his inner experiences, and on his own terms. This quality or ability made him a rara avis in the Swedish psychiatric environment, and doctors and staff realised this early on.

In his literally fantastic drawings, Lindblad conveyed both the contents and emotional timbre of his dreams and visions. There seemed to be a vast inner world, a system, a coherent big picture, that Lindblad tried hard to express in both images and words. Often, these expressions have a distinctly spiritual content and symbolism. There is a kinship with Swedish mystic Emanuel Swedenborg (that Lindblad had read), along with the Bible and other esoteric texts. Often, Lindblad describes that his soul leaves his body and experiences things and beings – sometimes of a distinctly "spiritual," symbolic nature, and sometimes of a more chiseled out religious ditto (that is, clothed in Christian symbolism).

Early on at Konradsberg, Lindblad wrote *En avhandling om hur jag kände mig och om alla de andliga manifestationer, som jag upplevt*. ("A dissertation about how I felt and about all the spiritual manifestations I've experienced"). This was a handwritten manuscript that he offered to his doctors. The text was most likely used as a foundation or basis when doctors wrote about his specific case – as in Bror Gadelius's book *Det Mänskliga Själslivet*, 1921 ("The Human Soul-life").[1] Gadelius acknowl-

1 Gadelius, Bror, *Det mänskliga själslivet*, Hugo Gebers Förlag, 1921. This four volume study is focused specifically on mental disorders and contemporary art theory.

edged Lindblad's talents as an artist and established the expressions as stemming from Lindblad's "spirit world." In a later article from 1937, Gadelius slightly reversed the perspectives by writing that there was in Lindblad, "a hysteric and willed characteristic that feeds the visionary approaches and from these develop a chronic 'spirit-watching.'" No matter which perspective is "correct," it's easy to see that Lindblad was valuable and unique in so many ways. He created, formulated, preserved, and was more than willing to share his findings. This was very much Hugo Lindblad's quintessence; he wanted his art to be of help to others.

Perhaps we could also speculate that the positive acknowledgment he received from his texts and drawings became an incentive to create more of the same? And that his own apparent "systemisations" of psychic- and dream-worlds probably attracted more attention than his many one-off colourful cartoons of daily life at the hospital? Without a doubt, Lindblad became a contributing part of an environment that was genuinely interested in the machinations of the mind, and also in the relationship between very general concepts such as "creative genius" and "madness."

In 1957, Lindblad completed a manuscript called *A World of Spiritual Things*. It's a unique attempt to very clearly express his own experiences. In part text, in part drawings; in part a kind of self-analysis, in part a spiritual quest. It's elaborate, well-written, and clearly conveys Lindblad's need to express. As such, it could definitely be described as a cathartic work. But the fact that it's so well-written also makes the reading experience almost a literary one. Like a mix between a soul-searching journey and a modernist exploration of literary form, the manuscript conveys what I think is the key to Hugo Lindblad: his compelling coherence.

After his death in 1976, Lindblad's collections of writings and drawings (mainly collected in approximately 25 "dream books") were willed to various psychiatric libraries. His idea was that these dream books could be used for the benefit of psychiatric research; specifically focussing on the beneficial aspects of inpatient creativity. Since then, there have been attempts to publish and exhibit his work, but this has mostly been done within clinical environments. The few times parts of his work were made available in more public settings (such as at Kulturhuset in Stockholm in 1983, and at Waldemarsudde in Stockholm in 1991), the images were well received.

Unfortunately, much of Lindblad's work has now been lost; it was stored in a maze of archival bureaucracy and – so it would seem – general carelessness. Mere fragments remain in material that was produced at the times of the exhibitions. The most valuable solid piece is in the collection of psychiatric nurse Gunnel Svedberg, who not only met Lindblad on several occasions at the Beckomberga Mental Hospital in the 1960s, but who also became his friend. She also later on wrote an informative thesis about his life and work for Ersta Sköndal Högskola (2014).[2]

Whether Lindblad's writings and images are still of value to the clinical community, or nowadays fit more snugly into the occult or spiritual art of that era that has been so well-acknowledged recently via the massive international successes of fellow Swede Hilma af Klint, one thing is clear: Hugo Lindblad was an artist first and fore-

2 Svedberg, Gunnel, *Hugo Lindblads förlorade drömmar – om en patient i vetenskapens tjänst*, Ersta Sköndal Högskola, Stockholm, 2014.

most, and a patient and psychiatric helper second. The benevolence and real value lie in Lindberg's own acknowledgment of his art and many talents; not specifically that he was eventually quoted by the esoteric world of psychiatry.

That said, Lindblad's willingness to share his inner sphere and outer work has contributed to an encouragement within Swedish psychiatry to involve creative methods and therapies. In many ways, he became the late 20th century Swedish "poster boy" for promoting the great benefits of artistic expression. Not necessarily in the service of an extended clinical environment, but always in the service of one's own self-exploration and healing processes.

Excerpts from Hugo Lindblad's "A World of Spiritual Things:"

The world, in which we live is a very wondrous thing and there is much truth in the old saying that there is nothing new under the sun. Great civilisations have arisen and vanished in the mists of countless centuries and the countries of our planet have been inhabited by peoples of whom generally speaking we know but very little. They have completely disappeared but have left behind themselves faint traces of their lives in ruined buildings, in those things that the earth gives up year after year, and in inscriptions upon stones.

They have left us many proofs of their intense interest in unseen worlds. Their monuments and buildings in most instances are representative of the things they held in awe. And even in this very modern world of ours, we continue to stand in awe of the unseen. We wonder but fail to solve the great problem for we can only faintly penetrate the deep shadows which cover the unknown. But the shadows may perhaps be swept away and then we may see clearly those things which now appear to us hidden in unfathomable depths.

The inhabitants of this earth have always been intensely interested in everything appertaining to the mystic and the occult, things which are in fact invisible. Many persons in various countries have acted either as a link with our world and the beyond, as we call it, or have become prominent in such matters. If we refer to the Bible, we see that God warns us against listening to people of other worlds or seeking to communicate with them, for such people have the power not only to destroy the body but what is worse, to destroy the soul. There are, however, what we might call natural means, that is when information is obtained although it is not sought for. It may be obtained in a way which passes all understanding. For instance, a person may at some moment or the other have the power to see and hear things which he cannot clearly comprehend, but he can and will describe what he has heard and seen.

Many say it is the end. But no, it is not the end: ending this mere life on this earth of ours is not the end of the life of the soul, nor is it even the beginning. We have existed in other forms and in other surroundings. We can see how much people are unlike each other even though they are of the same mother and there is no mother on this earth who can say with any degree of certainty to what heights of knowledge and accomplishment her newly born offspring will rise. There is a certain power in the life of a child which even parents cannot influence. Why? Because it relates to things spiritual. We do not see it but notwithstanding it does exist. And the people say, whither? Whither? That is the question which will always remain so and which, not knowing everything, I cannot answer. My own mother was a woman of this earth but her forbears were at intervals gifted with the power to see into the unknown world. My grandfather one night saw with his own eyes a church filled with people from the unknown world. A lady present at the time was on the point of swooning when she heard music as if in the air, but which really came from the ghostly congregation in the church. This was in 1840 and there was no wireless then.

The fundamental point is the Invisible. I know quite well that such things do in fact exist, witness wireless, electric currents. But are we fully aware of their nature? We have yet to solve many problems regarding these powers before we can hope fully to understand. They are unfathomable. They are as infinite as the heavens above. Electric power as well as invisible power comes from a source of unending power. It is the basis in the construction of all things.

I have already told you that I had never gone far away from my material body. I had ordinary dreams in which I saw several things such as for instance a donkey which an aunt had given me and which I was surprised not to find in the morning when I awoke and so on. I was now destined to have further experiences. I began to walk out through the door, down the staircase to the outer hall into the street. When I arrived in the hall, I had to go down a staircase of some sixty steps which ran round a central stone column. I now endeavoured to walk down these steps but the unseen power who accompanied me did not approve of my intention and prevented me from doing so. Instead I was propelled with great speed over the top of the steps and heard a very peculiar sound, something like clattering over stones. The sound was quite clear to me. I passed straight through the outer door into the street. I looked for the wire and saw that it came from the house and it swayed slightly as I stood at the side of the door close to the stone wall. It was as thin as an ordinary rubber band and continued to follow me as I began to walk along the street. For some minutes I saw nobody at all. I felt the wire and found that it was as strong as if made of iron. I pulled at it and found it was as elastic as rubber and when I let go, it went back to its previous position. The thought came into my mind to use my power of thought to convey me to some other place. I remembered a place where there was a lock on the river which I passed every day and with which I was quite familiar. In the space of a second, I was conscious that I was about to experience some kind of sensation. My brain was as if it were dimmed and in a partly conscious manner I found myself in the space of a second precisely at the spot about which I had thought. The time of transition was so short that the thought had not entirely left my brain when I arrived at the place in question.

On another occasion during the night when my spirit body was in bed I perceived something which closely resembled a mist which swayed to and fro from left to right and vice versa. Then it began to move up and down. It was a kind of luminous body and it stood out clearly against the darkness of the room. After examining it for some seconds, I noticed that there were many lines on the mist and finding this very strange, I examined it more closely. It was then that I saw that it was some kind of ornamentation which repeated itself over the whole mist at regular intervals. A few seconds passed and the mist stood out clearer than ever. The ornamentation was exactly like that of a honeycomb, six sided as in my sketch, and covered the whole of the mist. I subsequently went to sleep again, but I saw this wondrous mist many nights afterwards. One particular night when my spirit body awoke, I specially noticed that each of these six sided figures had a black spot in the middle from which delicate lines ran to the external corners. From now onwards I often saw these misty formations in broad daylight. It constituted part of my education which I am relating for the first time in my life. I have seen many of my visions in this mist and it formed a part of everything I saw in my dreams, but being finer than even the finest spider's web, it did not in any way detract from the clarity of the figures or brilliance of the light which I perceived.

It was now time for me to revert to my sleeping material body although I was not aware that it was so. I was anxious to remain in this delectable spot, but despite my desire to remain, the time for me to return had come. The spirit departed from the place at a great speed and I perforce was compelled to follow. My own power was impotent and I had to follow him. In the space of a second, I was again transported to the place from whence I had come, namely to the transparent glassy sea. I looked down and found the glassy surface under my feet, but my companion had completely disappeared. In a few seconds, I discovered myself speeding as if impelled by some inner power over a great area of glass and eventually came to a place where there was a great abyss. I stood at the edge and gazed down into the unfathomable depths. I became dizzy and knew not what to do. Then the idea came to me that I must go down into this abyss and I then saw a staircase leading down into its depths. I experienced the distinct feeling that this was the only way in which I could leave the barren glassy sea, for I could no longer see the mountain and its surroundings. All I could see was a desolate sea of glass extending away into the infinite and over all the bluish-yellow glow and the brilliant sun. I ventured on to the first step of the staircase and held on to the sides of the abyss. I began to descend but I kept my eyes closed, for I dared not look down into the unfathomable depths. When I had proceeded a little way down this ladder or staircase, I looked up and saw above me a great globe outlined in the bright yellow light which disappeared in the distance with a strange mellow bluish colour like that of crystal glass. I looked down and saw beneath me the great depths of the abyss and I noticed that I had still a long way to go, for the staircase seemed to disappear into space. This thought so unnerved me that I could scarcely support myself on the ladder and one of my hands missed its hold. At that precise moment, my whole body received an intense shock and I lapsed into unconsciousness. It was in this unconscious state that my body must have travelled at a tremendous speed back to earth, but how, I cannot say, for I was unconscious.

As I have related before, everything I saw was decked with ornaments and carvings, all of which were indeed very wonderful. It is difficult to describe these ornaments but I have no doubt that they were in fact destined for decorative purposes. I even saw such things in the underworlds. I have seen spirits whose hands were covered with some kind of ornaments which seemed to be embedded within the skin of their bodies. In the blue and green worlds there are very strange dogs and spirits of people much like bears, but as they seemed to be able to converse with each other, there is no doubt that they are in fact real spirits. I have illustrated one of these strange beings in a sketch. I am afraid I am unable to relate any more about these sinister worlds and will therefore conclude this part of my writings. It is not because I have nothing more to relate about these things, but because it would not serve any useful purpose, for I consider it best for all of us to consider more attentively the light world which is above us in the great invisible heavens. God indeed asked us to look up to Him and not down. I have myself suffered great anguish in my soul in regard to the evil of my life although I have lived a no worse life than the average human being. But the fact remains that there must have been some evil during my lifetime, for I have been transported to places which, as far as I am aware, no other person has seen. This gives me the feeling that I am very much like a hermit. I am entirely alone in this world and alone I shall remain but for the omnipotent power of the Lord God Almighty.

I fall asleep because I am tired, I undress and get into bed, I look at my watch and notice it is say 11.50 p.m. and I go to sleep. I cannot state the precise time I fall asleep, neither can anyone, for it is an unconscious act. In my dream I hear the clock on the wall strike midnight as I think. I am unconscious a second or so but I hear the chimes and begin to count them: one, two, three, four, five, six and •••••• but that is the end. I at once wake up and rushing from my bed find it is six o'clock whereas my original thought was twelve o'clock. At first I thought that it was the final chimes of midnight which I had heard, but when I look at my watch on the table, I find it says six o'clock in the morning. As sleep is an unconscious act, I must have slept the hours between at some tremendous speed. Does time really exist? I have discovered that time does not exist in dreams or in the spirit-worlds. It is only in our earthly world that we have discovered time, but there is a deeper meaning in the non-existence of time.

In order to gape into the unknown world, a person must obviously be endowed with special perception. I sincerely hope that the drawings which I give will supplement the written matter, and that you, my dear readers, will form your own unbiassed opinion therefrom. It may be that you have perhaps experienced the things which I relate, either in your dreams or in moments of wakefulness, for it is during the latter time that my dreams come to me entirely unbidden. If so, I will demonstrate to you in the pages which follow that there is at least something to be gained out of it all. The extent of these unseen worlds is great and the wonders thereof so marvellous that it is practically beyond the powers of feeble humanity to describe them with any degree of understanding and comprehension. You may, therefore, find that my drawings leave but a faint impression in your mind, for I cannot depict accurately what I have seen, for the colours and lights of this earth are not those of the unseen worlds. Everyone knows that the body is a material thing. We can feel it and see it. We can see other people and what they do. We can see the trees, the seas, and the land, the sun, the moon and the stars. But we cannot see the essence of the body, the trees, the earth or the flowers. We cannot see its real life because it is spiritual.

[Note: On the following pages, we can see some of the images from Lindblad's *A World of Spiritual Things*. I would like to thank Gunnel Svedberg for making this material available to me. / CA]

Mannen i stålvalvet.

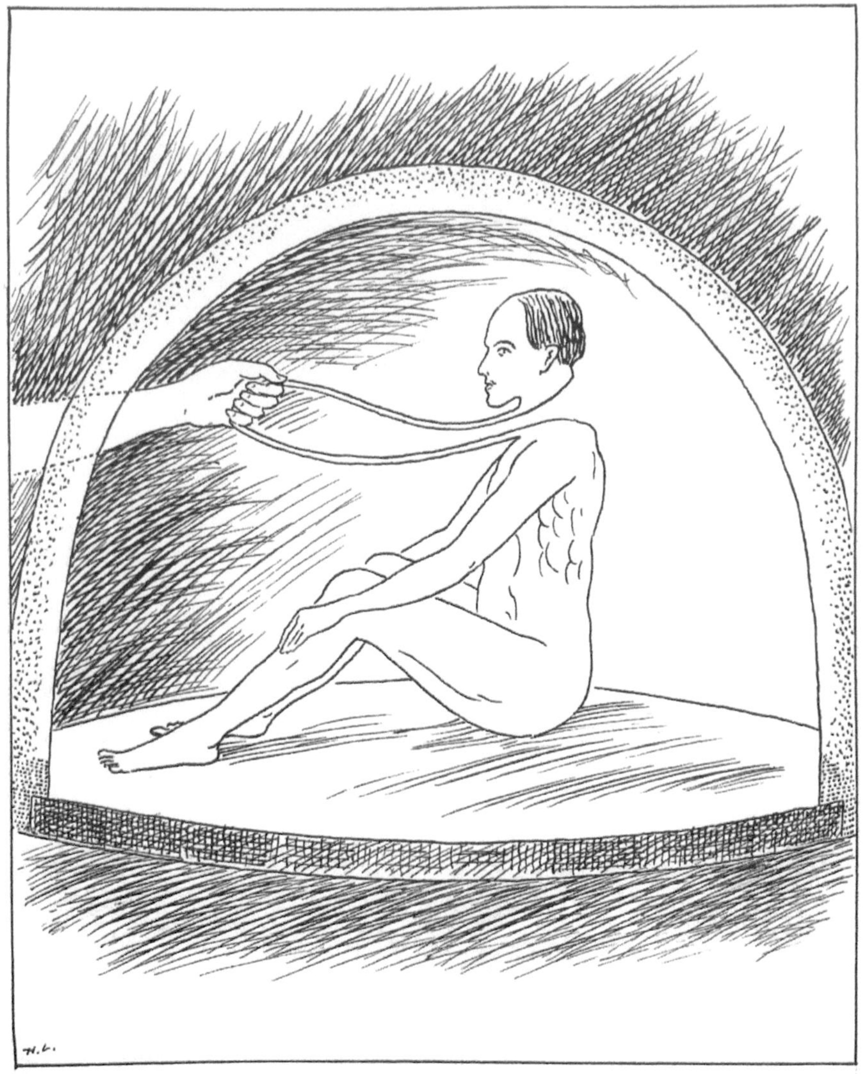

The man in the steel-vault.

Skuggan skymtar
vid min vänstra
axel.

Taktil hallucination
i verklig syn. Beröring
med starka pulsslag.

The shadow is dimly
seen at my left
shoulder.

Tactil hallucination
in real sight. Connection
(touch) with strong
beats of the pulse.

Schematisk bild av världar:
A. och B. = Högre Ängel-andars världar. Ljusvärldarna.
C. = Vår jord och dess andevärld.
F.1. = Människa. F.2. = Hav. F.3. = Ande.
D. = Den blå undervärlden med andar.
E. = Den gröna undervärlden med dess mystiska andar och kräldjur.

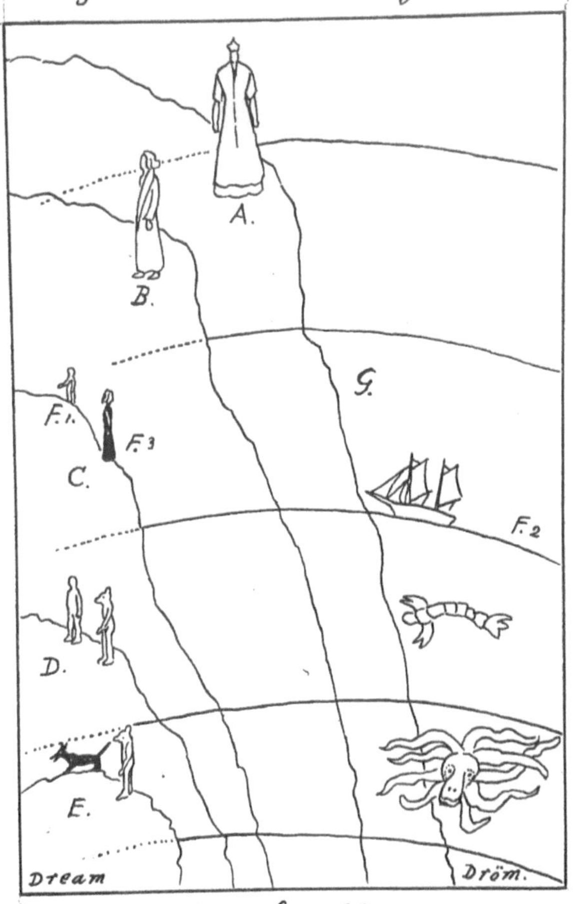

Schematic picture of worlds:
A. and B. = Worlds of higher Angel-spirits. Lightworlds.
C. = Our Earth and its spiritworld. F.1. = Man
F.2. = Sea. F.3. = Spirit.
D. = The blue underworld with spirits.
E. = The green underworld with its mystic spirits and reptiles.

1. Människo-Anden och tråden.
2. De två Andarna med trådar.

A.= The thread. (The chord). A.= Tråden. (Strängen)

1. The Man-Spirit and the thread.
2. The two Spirits with threads.

Andekraft stöter ut andekroppen från sidan.
A.= Andekropp. B.= Tråden. C.= Schikt varpå tråden flyter. D.= Andekraft i skepnad. E= Handen. F.= Materiekropp. G.= Stöt i sidan

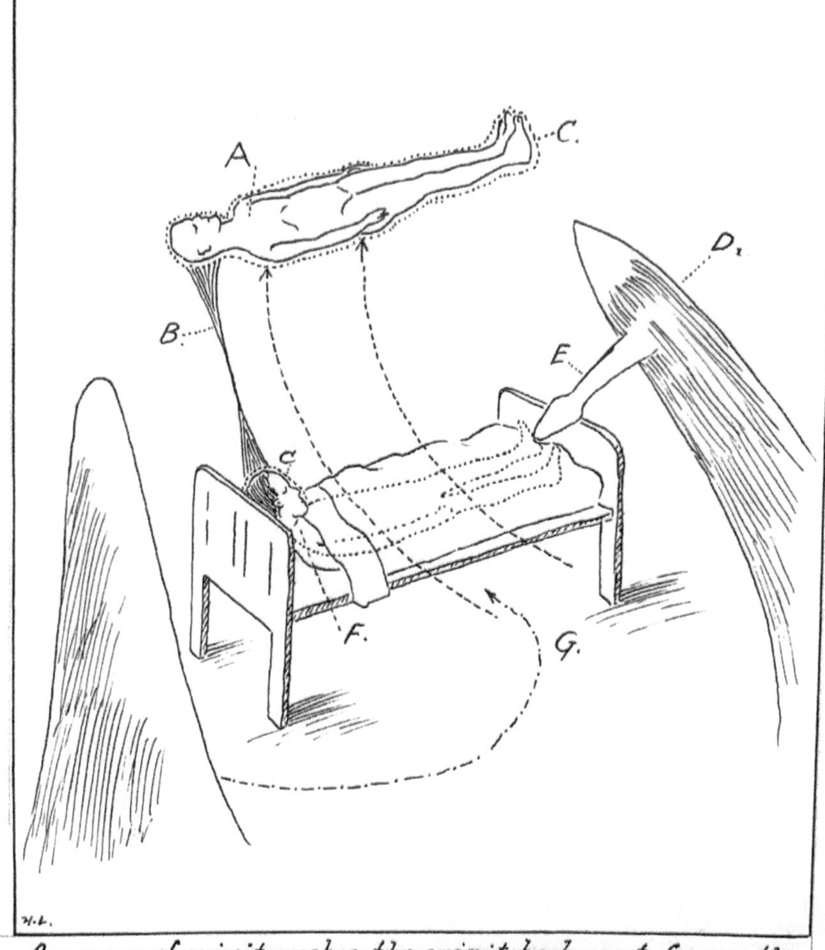

A power of spirit pushes the spirit-body out from the side.
A.= Spirit-body. B.= The thread (the cord). C.= Layer upon which the thread floates. D.= Power of spirit (in shape). E.= The hand. F.= Material body. G.= Push in the side.

Anden över den sneda skuggan.

The spirit over the oblique shadow.

De blå andarna på gatan av glas.

The blue spirits on the street of glass

Människan uppväckt i anden.
A.= Den sovande människan. B.= Den upp-
väckta anden.

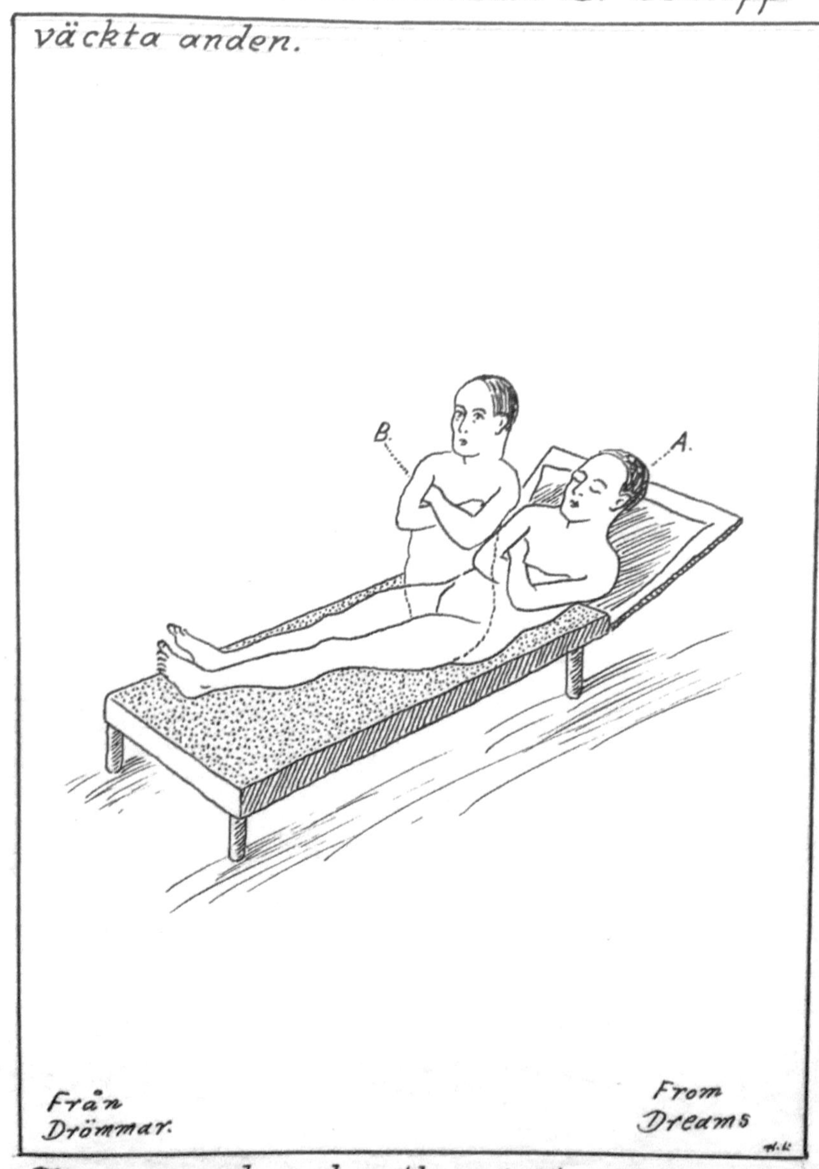

The man wakened in the spirit.
A.= The sleeping man. B.= The wakened
spirit.

Den konformade skuggan giver schock.
A.= 1:a Läget B.= 2:a Läget.

The cone-shaped shadow gives a chock.
A.= 1:st Situation. B.= 2:nd Situation.

De elektro-magnetiska strömmarna från öronen till bakhuvudet. A.= Yttre tryck.

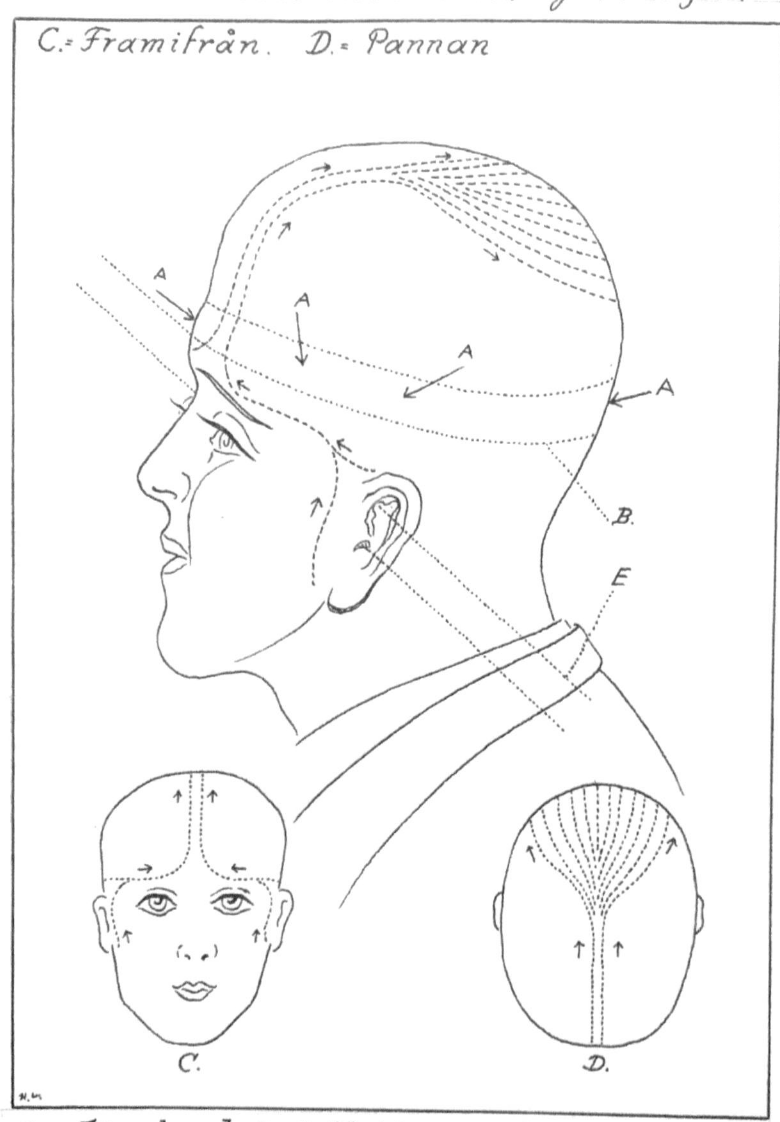

B = Järn-band. E= Stålstång. C= From in front.
D.= Forehead. A.= Outer pressure. B.= Iron-band.
E.= Steelbar (pole).
The electro-magnetic currents from the ears to the back of the head.

Playing with the Universe

Val Denham

The outsider artist does not need to be loved, appreciated, or even understood.

The outsider artist does not need to exhibit or sell work

The outsider artist works alone in a time and space of their own creation.

Children draw and paint. They think of this activity as playing. Then children grow up and forget to indulge themselves in the therapeutic rituals of innocent mark making. The outsider artist is an adult and a child in one entity. The process of making images, writing or making music is a means of controlling a hostile universe. For me, this practice is a form of psychic medication. All around me is chaos that needs to be tamed. Cleaning, placing objects in order, employing horizontal and vertical angles, making everything neat and tidy within my environment. It is why I love the blank rectangle of paper or canvas. A world of my own devising is contained. It cannot escape. Like a prehistoric fly in amber, it has been caught forever. I create order.

For 43 years, I never bothered to show my artwork to anyone. Not my family or my friends. Why would I? They wouldn't be interested and they would only think that I was even crazier than they imagined. Though, thinking back there was one exception during that time. I did have a solo exhibition in 1987 at a short lived gallery in London initiated by the Some Bizzare record label. It was only for one week. I had to be persuaded to do it. I was very reluctant. I have never done one again. Then I went back to total obscurity and the comfort and safety of my privacy. That is until recently, when through social media, I have shared some of my work, which has led to my work entering the public sphere, whilst I hide behind the pages of books, the laptop screen and the cameras and audio equipment of visiting friends. People have again asked me to exhibit. I do not do so.

I have always churned out creative endeavors, usually on a weekly basis. I don't have to, I just feel compelled. This Tranart, as I have named my creative output, most often than not, stems from my subconscious and my conscious mind working in harmony. The simple act of repetitive actions contained within the two dimensional miniature universe is pleasurable and to me; it is a therapeutic activity on many levels. Perhaps one difficulty in the creation of artworks is not quite knowing when to stop. I have been known to overwork things. Recurring themes manifest themselves naturally. My brain seems obsessed with certain themes to do with gender and mortality and this infatuation becomes exteriorized in familiar Tranart leitmotifs.

The Janus images, the endless self-portraits, the reproductive organs, the religious imagery, the demons and the angels. These symbolic representations are the specters of my own psyche.

The outsider artist is usually self-taught, innately talented yet quite often dysfunctional in society. Outside the mainstream, they are unconcerned with everyday realities such as financial reward or fame. The outsider artist will continue to produce visionary imagery in abundance regardless of any commercial remuneration or personal acclaim.

Society demands that we at least give the appearance of rationality. We are expected to say the appropriate things and to behave in a conventional manner. For some individuals, responding to society's artificially constructed and rigid expectations is uncomfortable and at times too difficult to maintain. The creative process can be an escape from the façade of normality. The outsider artist can be as unhinged as he or she wishes within the confines of the divine empty rectangle. It can be a relief to dissolve oneself into the subconscious realms of dream imagery, an art without rules or logic. There is no incentive for an outsider artist to explain intellectually a rationalization or a modus operandi for the benefit of a viewer. Why bother to explain one's intuitive compulsions to others, where is the benefit?

> 'We understand by this term works produced by persons unscathed by artist culture, when mimicry plays little or no part… These artists derive everything – subjects, choice of materials, means of transposition, rhythms, styles of writing, etc. – from their own depths, and not from the conventions of classical or fashionable art. We are witness here to the completely pure artistic operation, raw, brute, and entirely reinvented in all of its phases solely by means of the artists' own impulses. It is thus an art that manifests an unparalleled inventiveness.'
> (Dubuffet J. (1949) quoted in Rhodes C. (2000) p.24)

It is a mistake to believe that all outsider art is either primitive or childlike in its eventual form. Quite often this type of work can be sophisticated and anything but childlike in its complexity. There are inevitably recurring elements in many of these works such as esoteric symbolism, anthropomorphic creatures, and enigmatic phantoms that dissolve into the infinite patterns of the untamed imagination. Sometimes absurd pseudo-scientific principles and diagrams take precedence within the work. Repetitive mark making and hand written texts are commonplace to many outsider artists. Obsessions manifest as recurring motifs, often covering every particle of paper, canvas or even sculpture. The void must be destroyed, avoid a void, virgin paper or canvas is somewhat disturbing to the outsider artist. Vibrant colours redolent of psychedelic experiences can grow like ectoplasmic weeds across the artwork. This may be the result of manias or perhaps a serotonin imbalance. The artist is taking a drug free trip into the two dimensional confines of paper and canvas or the three dimensions of sculpture, these are the realms of the unreal. All these creative symptoms of mental illness can be both beautiful and psychologically illuminating to the

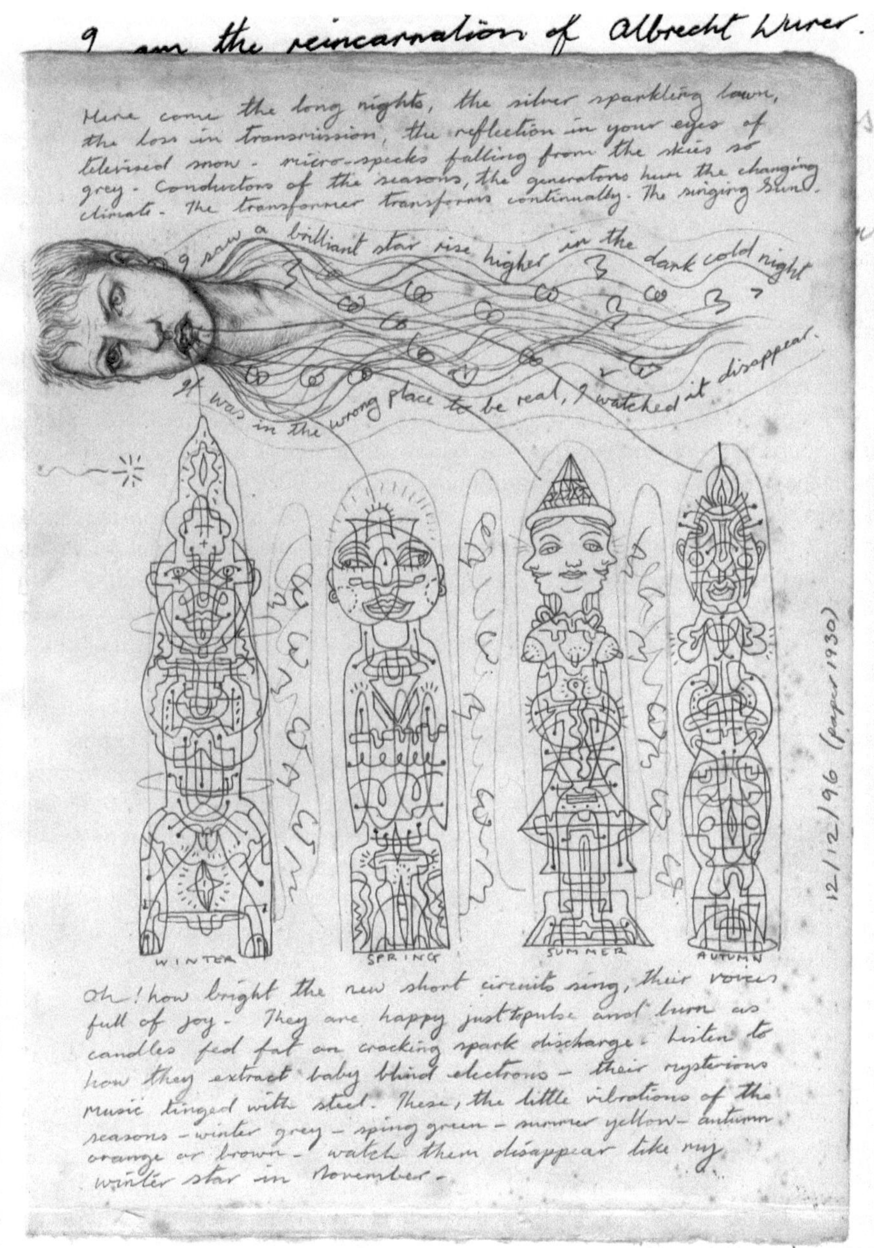

Art by Val Denham

viewer. The divine marriage of both the conscious and subconscious, resulting in new otherworldly esoteric information, purely for the benefit of the artist, this is art as medicine.

A typical artist of the outsider genre is Henry Darger. In 1973 it was discovered, as Darger lay in hospital in the final days before his death, that he had amassed a massive body of work in his tiny, dark and antiquated flat. Nathan Lerner, a photographer and designer, was given the task of clearing Darger's flat in Chicago. What he discovered was truly shocking. Darger, it appeared, had started work on a monumental book of over 15,000 typed pages in fifteen volumes. This gigantic work was started around 1910 and was based on the themes of war, weather conditions and the sufferings of innocent children at the hands of an evil army of grown men entitled *The Story of the Vivian Girls in what is known as The Realms of the Unreal, of the Glandeco-Angelinnean War storm, caused by the Child Slave Rebellion.* At some point Darger decided to illustrate scenes from the book. Nathan Lerner found 87 large watercolours, some nine feet long, crudely stitched together to make three very large books, and 67 smaller drawings. Many of the works were double sided with strange scenes set in idyllic surroundings often with little girls being strangled or dismembered by barbaric soldiers. Darger was not an accomplished draughtsman and felt that it would be better to trace images from magazines, mail order catalogues, comics or books, which he would then colour in with cheap children's watercolour paints. Darger, it seemed, was stealing art materials from the school where he worked as a janitor. Often, for some bizarre reason his little girls had penises. Gender transformation being another favourite outsider artist theme. Darger's huge output was never meant to be displayed or reproduced. He obsessively created this strange fantasy world purely for his own fulfilment. When Darger was in hospital he expressly asked for the books to be destroyed. What use could they serve to anyone else? His wishes were ignored. The work is displayed all over the world, it has been reproduced in many art books and now commands very high prices among passionate collectors. Some outsider art has become much sought after and collected within the rapacious art market, even though this was never the intention of the outsider artists themselves in the first place. Was it right to ignore Darger's dying wish? It is debatable.

Art as a therapeutic tool

The suppression of irrational behaviour, due to mental imbalance, within the confines of an artificially constructed normalcy in a civilised society, can be likened to a psychological straight jacket. The strange or eccentric behaviour of those individuals suffering (or blessed?) with mental health complications can be disturbing to the majority of approved reasonable people within conventional society. However, within the realms of creative endeavour, a total abandonment of reason can be beneficial to the artist and even therapeutic. Such work is also often admired and respected by many rational individuals and revered by those people interested in unconventional inventiveness within creative production. It is though a mistake to believe that all

Art by Val Denham

creative endeavours are therapeutic. Often making artworks is an escape from reality into another world, but for some, this other world is not always a welcoming one. It is quite possible to create artworks whilst feeling intense dysphoria or anxiety. The artwork itself can be a catalyst to melancholy or frustration for the creator of the work. One defining characteristic of outsider art particularly is a ceaseless compulsion to repeat certain motifs and pattern making. This type of art can be often obsessively overworked by the artist. Unable to stop making marks long after fatigue has set in; overworking so that an alien density is in danger of eating the artist. Adding written words to solidify and perpetually cage the demons hidden inside the two dimensional alternative universe forever is the only answer. A kind of exorcism through art, killing strange monsters with a paintbrush. Also, it is interesting to note that an artwork, or even a body of work that is interesting in psychiatric terms, may not necessarily be interesting as aesthetically competent art. Not all outsider artists who use the creative process as a therapeutic tool are competent or even interesting artists. There has to be at least some kind of visual talent inherent in the creator of the work for it to be aesthetically interesting.

Some of my own work may use motifs or obscure language, sometimes even using my own private code called 'The Cypher of Venus Castina'. This is done as a form of protection, or to hide in plain sight, that information which forms my own cosmology. Why would anybody wish to decipher my inner thoughts anyway? I still don't really understand myself. I'm not so much revealing my own universe as discovering it myself. I'm an explorer of my own brain. I give small glimpses of this universe every now and then through my Tranart, which includes visual work, audio recordings and text. The one defining characteristic of all my creative output is a compulsion to produce objects, texts or sounds which are fixed permanently in the real world. This is directly connected to my own obsessive compulsive behaviour. I'm trying to create order in a chaotic universe. I often feel anxious or uncomfortable if I am not involved in either domestic cleaning duties or creating art. Without a doubt, my major compulsion is to clean and continually order objects around our house. I have a compulsion to make sounds, or to manifest into the real world the music that is playing in my head. The only remedy for these afflictions is concentrating on an artistic project, or losing myself in my collection of vintage horror film magazines. Life is very wonderful. I wouldn't change a thing.

(2020)

Bibliography

– Rhodes, C. (2000) *Outsider Art: Spontaneous Alternatives*, London, Thames and Hudson.

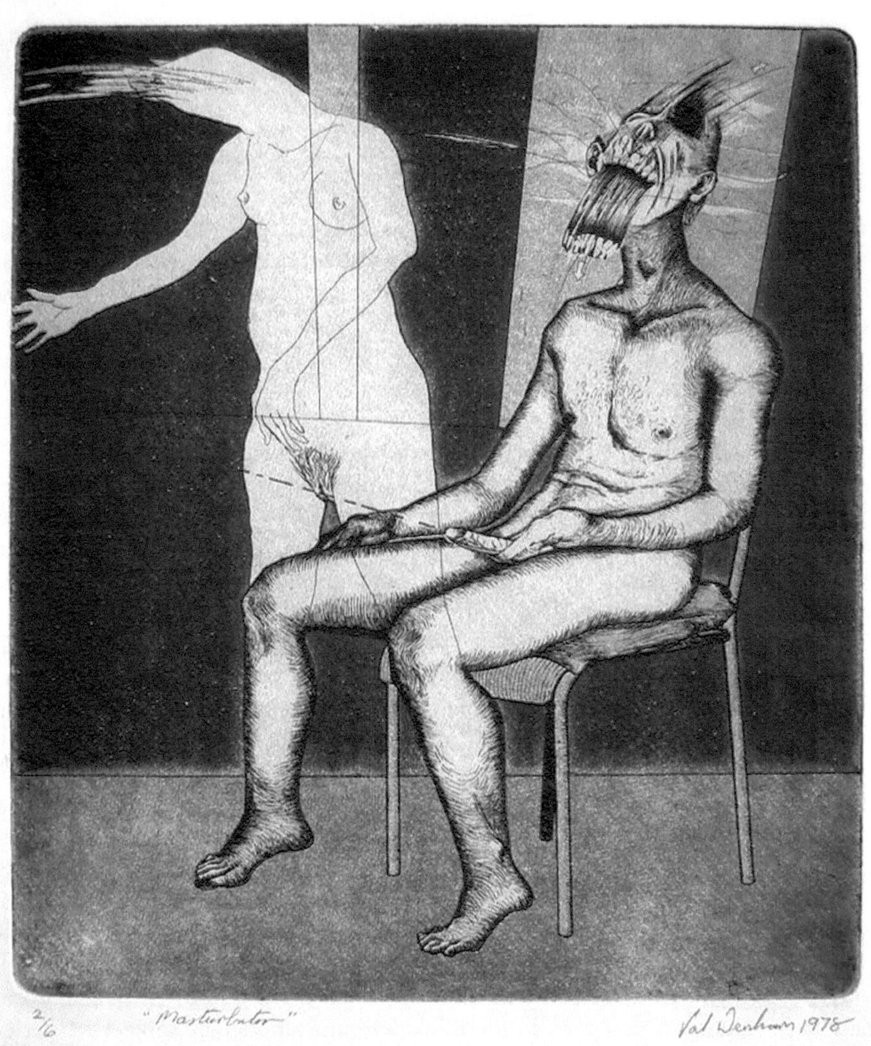

Art by Val Denham

Outsider/Inpatient: Creativity & Mentabolization

Vanessa Sinclair

We are born into a story, an already existing narrative. Even before we are born, our parents, family and society have ideas of who we will be, what we will do, how we will succeed, and what trials we may face, all before we have even left our m/others' body. Our identity is prescribed, in utero, and not with us in mind. It is mapped out for us, structured, put into play, and is largely based on gender. The first question asked of us, "Is it a boy or a girl?" leaves no room for ambiguity – boys have penises, girls do not. And although we are all well aware of the atrocities that can take place in the early assignment of gender to children born intersex, and what catastrophic repercussions this often has, rather than exalt the hermaphroditic, as has been done in times past, we continue to force people into categories we've deemed socially acceptable. The system is built on dichotomy: male/female, active/passive, 1/0, master/slave. But what happens when we begin to break down this system, push boundaries, surpass borderlines and transgress limits?

At the turn of the twentieth century, Sigmund Freud released his seminal work, *Three Essays on the Theory of Sexuality* (1905), in which he introduced his theory of childhood sexuality, outlining the oral, anal and genital stages for the first time, claiming we are all born bisexual and intrinsically polymorphously perverse. The expert on sexuality and perversions at the time was Richard von Kraft-Ebbing, who believed – as did society at large – that sex is solely for procreation, and any sexual act falling outside of the reproductive intention was considered to be perverse. Freud actually agreed with this definition of perversion but stated that perversion is our natural inclination; it is the norm and even precedes what we consider to be "norms."

Humans are sexual beings. Children are sexual beings. We are all perverse, and the entire body is sexual, not just the genitals and erogenous zones. Any part of the body can become eroticized, as can the gaze, smell or voice. Sexuality and sexual identity can change over a person's lifetime or circumstances. The subject is inserted into h/er sexual nature. Attempts to grasp onto an identity can be seen as one grappling with sexuality, with one's intrinsic sexual nature, attempting to categorize it, restrict it, contain it, and give it a limit in an effort to control it.

Freud (1923) stated our ego is first and foremost a body-ego. We learn about ourselves and the world via our bodies, especially through our orifices, as these are the spaces where we exchange inside and out, ingest and discharge, are penetrated and expel. These sites are holes, openings, gaps, but also limits, boundaries and surfaces; the rim of the mouth, anus, urethra, vagina, nostrils, eyes and ears. We may even consider the pores of the skin to be countless numbers of orifices, tiny mouths opening and closing more quickly or slowly depending on our state, mood, level of stimulation or relaxation.

For Jacques Lacan, identity/ego is first formed during the mirror stage. During this time (ages 6-18 months), the child experiences he/r self and body as fragmented, but when s/he sees he/r self in the mirror, the mirror image appears to be whole. As the child's experience of he/r own body/self is fragmented, there seems to be a disconnect between one's experience of one's self and the image in the mirror. This experience of disconnect continues throughout life. Through this process of identification, the child is able to internalize the cohesive sense of self that s/he imagines the mirror image to have, which thus forms the ego/identity. We identify with what we imagine ourselves to experience. The ego/identity is therefore an identification with a fantasy. However, the position of what would more accurately be considered to be the true self, what Lacan calls the subject, is not equivalent to the ego/identity but rather is situated in the gap that exists between consciousness and matter, the ego and the real of the body, perception and the unconscious.

We can see this fantasy of cohesion break down in psychosis, for example, where the person is plagued by the experience of the fragmented body/self and unable to pull he/r consciousness out of the real of the body and into the realm of the imaginary, which makes the experience of living more tolerable via fantasy. Another realm in which we gain a glimpse of our real fragmented state is in our dream lives. Here we often experience a state of anxiety accompanied by pieces of a puzzle, which we later string together upon retelling in an attempt to form a cohesive narrative. We actually perform a similar action in our waking lives as well, as our waking lives are also a series of disjointed events that we string together via fantasy to create an experience of a cohesive narrative that we then relate to ourselves and others.

It is useful to view waking and dream states not as a binary of awake-asleep but rather a continuum of wakefulness-sleep/conscious-unconscious. In this way, we recognize that when we are asleep we oftentimes have "one eye open" and are able to perceive that which is happening in our environment. Often our dreams are a way to encourage ourselves to remain asleep. What we call our "psychic censor" decides not only what will be allowed from the unconscious into consciousness – however altered it is in representation to veil its true meaning – but also masks stimuli from the environment, frequently incorporating it into the dream work (i.e. when an alarm clock becomes a fire alarm in our dream and we suddenly need to evacuate the building). Similarly, when we are "wide awake" our unconscious mind is still active and is more or less present in daydreams, fantasies, imagination, etc. This concept of the ratio or continuum in a state of flux can be applied not only to dream-wake states and conscious-unconscious but also to aspects of identity such as gender and sexuality.

In his paper, *Gender, Sex and the Sexual* (2003/2011), Jean Laplanche differentiates gender, sex and sexuality in the following way: Gender is plural. It is oftentimes seen as dual, as in masculine-feminine, but it is not so by nature. It is actually plural, existing on a continuum. Sex is dual. It is so by virtue of sexual reproduction and also by virtue of its human symbolization, which sets and freezes the duality as presence/absence or phallic/castrated. The sexual is multiple, polymorphous. The fundamental discovery of Freud, it is based on repression, the unconscious and fantasy. It is the object of psychoanalysis.

The drive as Freud posits it lies somewhere between the body and the mind, on the border. The drive never works on the whole body or whole subject and therefore is always focused on fragments or individual activities, together with a quality of being active or passive. Drives are always partial, and we all have varying combinations of these partial drives. Therefore, a catalog of drives is impossible because everyone develops their own unique combination of variations.

Ultimately every human being could be described as perverse. But why don't we remain "perverse"? Because we all go through a process of normalization via socialization in childhood. This normalization process is also known as the Oedipus complex. However, normalization fixes desire. It constrains the mobility of desire, orienting it in increasingly limiting ways – you must desire persons, specifically persons of the opposite sex, then only certain sexual acts with a certain person of the opposite sex. This freezes fragments of the unconscious evermore into what we call an identity. Defining what you are, who you are, how we can categorize you so that we may separate ourselves from you… you are not like us, you have an illness, a disease, you are an addict, an other. If we pin down the problem, we can prescribe a solution. The over-pathologization of the human experience. However, normalization fails. All paths that sexuality, drive and desire may take are equally valid and complex. In fact, Lacan called the hetero-normative prototype, "the delusional normality of genital relations."

The Oedipal complex is the process through which everyone works in order to move from a dynamic of two to three positions. This enables one to break away from the mirror relation with the other and turn towards a third. Once this is achieved, one may then slide metonymically into the position of the other, and then again into the position of the third, thereby enabling the possibility of assuming each and all positions. This movement or metonymy is essential.

A characteristic of human desire is that it can never be wholly fulfilled, and therefore lends itself to constant momentum or movement. Freud posited that the ultimate goal was genital primacy, but through the work of Lacan, this has since been realized to be an absurd notion, as each and every path that a drive takes is as equally valid as any other. The goal of desire is to go on desiring.

Identity itself is a regulatory norm. The concept of the individual is a product of power. Freud's conceptualization of the subject as divided (conscious/unconscious) undermines the possibility of a seamless identity, sexual or otherwise. Identity is illusory. Historicism relegates identity to cultural and social practices. A society's ideology of individuality ensures maximum freedom as long as one conforms.

Our ego is the internalized ideal of our parents, as was theirs and those before that, connecting one dimension of social identification/exclusion with another through generations. As Tim Dean writes, queer theory and politics began with a critique of identity and identity politics. Queer is opposed to normalization and attempts to evade the impasse of identity politics.

In his book *What is Madness?* (2011), Darian Leader notes that when we think of madness and treating psychosis, what we are really concerned with is returning patients back to what is considered to be the social norm. In this book, he gives an example of a patient he was working with that seemed no different than many of his friends. He was thoughtful and engaging, studied philosophy and psychology. When Leader asked the staff why this person was interned in a long-term mental health care facility, they seemed to look at him like he hadn't figured it out yet. Eventually, in one of their sessions, the patient began talking about some other planet he lived on that was not Earth. The patient's affect didn't change, he was not distressed. He spoke about this place like it was any other fact of life. While Leader understood that this discrepancy between the patient's personal reality and the agreed upon consensus reality of society meant this patient had a "delusion," he didn't seem to think it warranted someone having to live in an inpatient facility the rest of their lives.

Working in government run hospitals in New York City, I have encountered similar experiences. What if, instead of automatically pathologizing the experiences of others who are not like us, instead we provide room for them and their symptom, in an understanding that the symptom is in place for a reason? It is holding the person together, buttressing them in some way that is fundamental to their functioning, and therefore should be respected and supported, not pathologized, belittled or ridiculed.

Dutch painter Vincent van Gogh (1853-1890) is one of the seminal figures in the development of modern art, and the classic example of a "genius madman," whose work, ideas and way of being was shunned in his community during his lifetime. Van Gogh's trajectory caused a shift in the art world that has caused art brokers and curators to be forever scouting for such an outsider artist, lest another go unnoticed or be tossed aside in our times.

Van Gogh worked with such fervor at an intense pace, resulting in the creation of almost 900 paintings in less than a decade.[1] Throughout his life, van Gogh was hospitalized for periods of time during epsiodes of mental decompensation and extreme duress, and was known to have frequent outbursts and altercations in pubs and public in the villages in which he lived.

Van Gogh's innovative brushstrokes and use of color revolutionized painting. His short, thick applications of paint were unlike any before and remain unlike any since. His use of color and light was unconventional, reflecting the play of light in the natural world; highlighting the motion of light like waves pouring over his scenes, whether these be fields of wheat, rolling hills, distant towns, flowers, empty rooms, or people. Van Gogh brought together fragments of paint in such a way, combining color, form and texture to create his idiosyncratic view of the scene at hand. Van Gogh was able to mix his inner world with the outer reality, merging impressions from the surrounding environment with internal experiences and sensations. When standing before his artworks, one can almost feel the anxiety and

1 "Vincent van Gogh Paintings," Van Gogh Gallery. Accessed November 20, 2019: https://www.vangoghgallery.com/painting/

intensity of emotion emanating from them.

Van Gogh documented his process, dreams, innermost thoughts and desires in his writings, often in the form of letters[2] to his brother Theo, which he wrote almost daily at times, as well as to friends and fellow artists. He expressed concern about how he would be received by others, and desperately hoped to one day be a recognized artist. Through his writing, we glean the inner experience of a man fighting for sanity and survival through the medium of his artwork. As opposed to modern day conceptual art, which is more of a thought-experiment emanating from the ego or conscious mind of the artist, van Gogh's work embodies the inherent function of the creation of art. Outsider art, what I would consider to be the truest form of art, is often compulsive, intense and fervent; born from a need that the artist has to bring he/r internal, unconscious experiences out onto the canvas (or whatever the preferred mode of working or material may be). Art is a way of working with and through unconscious material; a way of manifesting oneself, as well as the surrounding reality.

Through his letters, it is clear that van Gogh felt a compulsion to paint. He harbored an impulse to express himself and to share his view of the world with others. This desire reflects Freud's statement, "What grips us so powerfully can only be the artist's intention, in so far as he has succeeded in expressing it in his work and in getting us to understand it. I realize that this cannot be merely a matter of intellectual comprehension; what he aims at is to awaken in us the same emotional attitude, the same mental constellation as that which in him produced the impetus to create" (Freud, 1914, p. 212). In this way van Gogh wanted to impart the experience of life which ignited the creative spark within him.

The process of the creation of art is often a way to work with or through traumatic events or material in one's life, which might otherwise be left repressed or unsymbolized. "Do all you can to persevere in that which exceeds your perseverance. Persevere in the interruption. Seize in your being that which has seized and broken you" (Badiou, 2000, p. 47). Alberto Burri (1915-1995)[3] is another example of a person who worked through intense life events and experiences via his creative practice. Burri initially pursued the study of medicine, when he was called into military work. He was eventually captured and detained in an American internment camp for Italian prisoners of war, where he began to practice creating art. "I painted every day. It was a way of not having to think about the war and everything around me" (Braun, 2016, p. 30).

When art supplies in the prison camp were scarce, Burri worked with whatever materials he could find. He salvaged burlap sacks and stretched them into canvases. When he was finally released he returned to his native Italy, only to find his homeland completely destroyed. Historic cathedrals, irreplaceable monuments and buildings were demolished; homes, streets and squares in ruin. Burri continued his artistic practice. Utilizing burlap, earth, tar, pumice, sawdust, metals and plastics, Burri often incorporated found objects into his work. Sometimes he cut or burned his

2 "Vincent van Gogh: The Letters," Van Gogh Museum. Accessed November 18, 2019: http://vangoghletters.org/vg/letters.html

3 Biographical information from Braun, E. (2016). Alberto Burri: the Trauma of Painting. New York: Guggenheim.

pieces, creating these sorts of wounds in the works, which he would then suture with cord or twine. In this way, it seems as if Burri recreated the torn flesh of the soldiers through his work, and then healed them by sowing them back together:

> Burri saw (and heard) the carnage of war, but he also felt the bodily trauma of others. Doctors in the field suffered their own kinds of stress brought on by the challenge of operating nonstop, the responsibility for evaluating mental fitness in others, and the moral imperative to save lives… They were exposed to seemingly endless streams of bloodied bodies for which the only possible response was pragmatic and merciful acts of repair. (Braun, 2016, p. 36)

The lives of Leonora Carrington (1917-2011) and Max Ernst (1891-1976) were also inextricably affected by war. The couple first met at a dinner party in London in 1937, held in honor of the opening of a major exhibition of Ernst's work[4] and soon relocated to Paris. In her work, Carrington seamlessly mixes dream and reality, the magical and mundane, human and animal, natural and man-made; Ernst created collages to accompany Carrington's short stories, and the couple designed sculptures of humans with the heads of animals and animals with the heads of humans, which they installed as guardians and gatekeepers around their home, as well as throughout their garden. The artists often portrayed mythical and hybrid creatures as symbols of transformation. "Horses and birds, both of which had emerged prior to the couple's meeting, soon became talismans and transitional beings that challenged oppositional terms like male/female, animal/human, mythic/real. They were readily incorporated into both artists' mythologies of hybridity, androgyny and the surrealist couple; of individual freedom and psychic and physical transformation" (Chadwick, 2017, pp. 66-67).

Ernst opened up new areas through his work with collage. He combined photograph, image and word, at times adding drawings of his own to the cut-out images, as well as adding poetic inscriptions and titles. Ernst viewed his collage work as akin to automatic writing or drawing, as he often worked in an automatic fashion, feeling his works provoked unconscious imagery in the viewer; he described them as expressing the hallucinatory qualities of dreams. "Contradictory images, double, triple and multiple images, piling up on each other with the persistence and rapidity which are peculiar to love memories and visions of half sleep" (Ades, 1976, p.20). Ernst's works are dreamlike. There is a malleability and fluidity of personal traits as well as gender expressions and identities. Ernst even created entire collage novels, including *The Hundred Headless Woman* (1929), *A Little Girl Dreams of Taking the Veil* (1930), and *A Week of Kindness* (1934).[5] In analyzing *The Hundred Headless Woman*, M.E. Warlick (b. 1946) notes:

---

4 Biographical information tracing the relationship between Leonora Carrington, Max Ernst, Leonor Fini and Peggy Guggenheim culled from Chadwick, W. (2017). *The Militant Muse: Women of Surrealism.* London: Thames & Hudson. pp. 60-102.

5 "Max Ernst's Collage Novels Are Part Séance, Part Victorian Underworld, and All Uncanny," by Mark Dery. Hyperallergic. Accessed December 7, 2019: https://hyperallergic.com/424432/max-ernsts-collage-novels-are-part-seance-part-victorian-underworld-and-all-uncanny/

> One of these collages alludes to a central theme of the novel, the fluctuating genders of the principal characters between Loplop, the male bird, and La Femme, the hundred-headless woman. The caption to the collage "The Demi-fecund Ram Dilates Its Abdomen at Will and Becomes a Ewe" indicates this animal's magical ability to change from male to female. This transmutation is enacted in other ways throughout the novel, particularly in the sequential substitutions of male and female figures in similar poses… (2001, p. 111)

In 1939, Ernst was arrested as a German citizen in France. Hans Bellmer (1902-1975) was also interned in the same prison at the same time. "In Berlin before the War, German critics saw his work as 'degenerate' and pornographic - lacking the idealism of the Aryan creed. When Bellmer came to Paris in 1938, his problems with censorship followed as the Nazis came to occupy France" (Morgan, 1993, p. 286). Carrington spent months writing Ernst letters, bringing him gifts and meals. He was eventually released and able to return home for a time, and the couple returned to their creative life together - writing, painting, cooking and gardening - for a period.

However, Ernst was soon arrested and detained once more, and this time friends insisted Carrington leave France and flee to Spain. Upon arriving in Madrid, however, Carrington was abducted and raped by a group of Spanish soldiers. In distress, she fled to the British Consulate where, instead of receiving the help she sought, she was declared "mad"[6] and committed to a psychiatric hospital. Carrington outlined her anguish and mental decomposition in the book, *Down Below* (1975).

Hans Bellmer met his life partner and creative collaborator Unica Zürn (1916-1970) in the early 1950s. Zürn often modeled for Bellmer, her form bound and cut. Bellmer tied ropes around Zürn's nude body, cutting her flesh into distorted shapes and forms, often photographing her with truncated limbs and head; a fragmented torso perched upon a stool. The couple's work explored the dissociation and fragmentation of the body in a similar way that other artists explored the shattered world around them during the periods of the two World Wars through the cutting up of word, sound and image.

Upon meeting Zürn, Bellmer is said to have proclaimed, "Here is the doll."[7] Bellmer's first artworks involving the dismemberment and reassembling of dolls began in 1933. He described his first creation "Die Puppe" ("The Doll") as "an artificial girl with multiple anatomical possibilities,"[8] documenting the various stages of the doll's assembly and dismemberment in a book of the same name published the following year. In Bellmer's work, bodies are often presented disfigured, deconstructed and reconfigured in uncanny ways. He often photographed his dolls from odd angles, causing the audience to feel voyeuristic as we come upon the scene. Sometimes he placed emphasis on the breasts and genital areas of the mannequins.

---

6 Chadwick, W. (2017). *The Militant Muse: Women of Surrealism*. London: Thames & Hudson. p. 100.

7 "A stone for Unica Zürn." *Art in America*. Accessed August 23, 2019: https://www.artinamericamagazine.com/news-features/magazines/a-stone-for-unica-zurn/

8 "Hans Bellmer - Plate from La Poupée (1936)." MOMA. Accessed February 21, 2020: https://www.moma.org/collection/works/92611

> Bellmer's erotic imagination absorbed every aspect of his work, including the paintings, drawings, sculptures and photographs. His vision was a ravishing obsession, and his assiduity as an artist was consumed by an unremitting search for the heightened (and obscure) object of desire. In giving the Doll its variety of visually constructed permutations… Bellmer explored the outermost limits of sexual conflict and resolution, openly investigating the dark side of consciousness, the discomforting zone between Eros and Thanatos. (Morgan, 2013, p. 286)

This play with the parts of the body and dismemberment of the self via the double of the doll is reflective of the true state of being that underlies our unconscious fantasy of seamless self-cohesion and identity. Our underlying experience is one of disturbance, disjunction and fragmentation. Perhaps this is one reason why the masses find artwork that nods to this underlying experience, disturbing; it gives the viewer a glimpse into one's own state of mind, the state of mind-body experience that we have all worked our whole lives to smooth over and cover up.

In Bellmer's work the function of sublimation through the creation of art is apparent and a prime example of one of the many reasons why art should never be censored. Imagine if Bellmer had not had this creative outlet for his impulses and urges, and was unable to express them in an artistic way. Instead of suffering in isolation or potentially even inflicting harm, he was able to channel his impulses, creating strange, uncanny beauty in these provocative forms.

In in-patient psychiatric settings, we are able to see how creativity and the arts play a crucial role in containment, expression, metabolization and working through. A wonderful example of an in-patient/ outsider artist, who illuminates many of the concepts just discussed, is the Danish artist, Ovartaci.

Born in 1894, Ovartaci (then Louis Marcussen) was admitted to an inpatient hospital in 1929, after pointing a rifle at one of her blind brothers. She remained in forced hospitalization for 56 years. Ovartaci was extremely prolific for decades. She drew, painted and sculpted utilizing all sorts of materials, including fabric, cardboard, metal, plaster, *papier maché*, and wire. She painted the bed in which she slept, created smoking pipes using sardine cans, and life-size dolls. Through her work, she describes internal experiences, dreams, and past lives. She loved to tell imaginative stories that would drawn in the listener. Some staff would even bring their children into the ward on Sundays to listen to her tell her stories, enraptured.

The head psychiatrist allowed Ovartaci a single room, the freedom to refrain from psycho-pharmaceutical treatment, and the ability to create her artwork. However, at one point during her hospitalization, when she was relocated, she was met with resistance to her artwork by the new doctor and staff, and her work and art supplies were taken away from her in an attempt to "cleanse" her. This of course agitated her beyond consolation. She became catatonic and refused to eat. The staff eventually relented, returning her art supples and life-size sculptures to her.

Ovartaci often created creatures that seem to be a combination of human and animal. Usually the figures were visibly female, with painted lips and breasts, often seeming to vacillate between being apes, humans, fantasy fairytale creatures, and even extra-terrestrials. She created worlds filled with sprites, fairies, nymphs, panthers, tigers, birds, and flying machines. She often created Janus-headed figures, able to see both forward and backward at the same time, to see an issue from multiple angles. The Janus head symbolizes change and transition from one state to another – from one way of seeing to another. It is these transitional phases and different modes of being that Ovartaci so beautifully captures in her work. She often seems to describe or connote the process of transformation or evolution. It is notable that she often cut a hole where the genitals would be.

Identifying as a woman, and after requesting a sex change operation for years, in 1954, Ovartaci succeeded in amputating her own penis, utilizing a chisel from the hospital's carpentry workshop. Before that she had made an unsuccessful attempt with a razor blade. To prevent any potential problems or infection, she is then granted a proper sex change operation via a medical professional. After which time it is reported that she becomes visibly calmer, more content, more sociable, and less agitated.

I mention this brief overview of the life and work of Ovartaci, as one example of many, wherein life itself could be considered a work of art. She created constantly, compulsively, decorating everything around her. Her bed, her chair, her mirror. She created companions in these sculptural works and dolls. A fantasy world. A world of her own. Instead of pathologizing individuals like Ovartaci – who was not listened to, whose sense of self was negated, deemed to be pathological – what if we broaden our parameters of what is seen as socially acceptable, as is happening nowadays with regard to sexuality, gender identity and sexual orientation? If we recognize that all paths are equally valid, rather than seeing so many as "deviations from the norm." If we "give sanity a longer leash" so to speak and understand that *sinthomes* are in place for a reason. Rather than disturb or negate, what if we celebrate and support, respect our psychological and neurological differences, see our varying symptom formation as different ways of being in the world, rather than othering, separating ourselves, and locking individuals away? What if we think of our own lives as works of art that can be curated creatively? Everyone has the ability to be creative in some way. Whether this is through traditional fine arts, such as drawing, painting, photography and collage, or creating life-size sculptures, implements and worlds like Ovartaci, or through writing, poetry, music, gardening, wood-working, cooking, sewing, quilting… all of these methods *mentabolize*, making life more bearable, and should be encouraged and respected.

Bibliography

– Badiou, A. (2000). *Ethics: An Essay on the Understanding of Evil.* New York: Verso.
– Bellmer, H. (1969). *Oeuvre Gravé.* Paris: Editions Denoël.
– Bellmer, H. (2004). *Little Anatomy of the Physical Unconscious or the Anatomy of the Image.* Waterbury Center, VT: Dominion Publishing.
– Braun, E. (2016). *Alberto Burri: the Trauma of Painting.* New York: Guggenheim.
– Butler, J. (1990). *Gender Trouble: Feminism and the Subversion of Identity.* London: Routledge.
– Carrington, L. (1988). *Down Below.* New York: New York Review of Books.
– Chadwick, W. (2017). *The Militant Muse: Women of Surrealism.* London: Thames & Hudson.
– Dean, T. (2000). *Beyond Sexuality.* Chicago: University of Chicago Press.
– Dean, T. (2006). "Lacan meets queer theory." In *Perversion: Psychoanalytic Perspectives, Perspectives on Psychoanalysis,* Dany Nobus & Lisa Downing (Eds.) London: Karnac Books. pp. 261-322.
– Ernst, M. (1929/2017). *The Hundred Headless Woman.* New York: Dover Publications.
– Ernst, M. (1930/2017). *A Little Girl Dreams of Taking the Veil.* New York: Dover Publications.
– Ernst, M. (1934/ 2017). *A Week of Kindness.* New York: Dover Publications.
– Freud, S. (1905). "Three essays on the theory of sexuality." *The Complete Standard Edition of the Psychological Works of Sigmund Freud (SE) VII.* London: Hogarth Press. pp. 123-246.
– Freud, S. (1914). "The Moses of Michelangelo." *SE XIII.* London: Hogarth Press. pp. 211-236.
– Freud, S. (1923). "The ego and the id." *SE XIX.* London: Hogarth Press. pp. 1-66.
– Iwaya, K. (2011). *The Doll: Hans Bellmer.* Tokyo: Éditions Treville.
– Lacan, J. (2006). "The mirror stage as formative of the I function as revealed in psychoanalytic experience." *Écrits: the First Complete Edition in English.* Translated by Bruce Fink. New York: W.W. Norton & Co. pp. 75-81.
– Lacan, J. (2016). *The Seminar of Jacques Lacan Book XXIII. The Sinthome* (1975-1976). Translated by A.R. Price. New York: W.W. Norton & Co.
– Laplanche, J. (2011). *Freud and the Sexual.* International Psychoanalytic Books.
– Leader, D. (2011) *What is Madness?* London: Hamish Hamilton.
– Lejsted, M. & Danielsen, E. (2014). *Ovartaci: In more Dimensions.* Denmark: Museum Ovartaci.
– Morgan, R.C. (2013). "Hans Bellmer – The Infestation of Eros." In Carl Abrahamsson (Ed.). *The Fenris Wolf, vol. 6.* Stockholm: Edda Publishing. pp. 285-293.
– Verhaeghe, P. (1999). *Love in a Time of Loneliness: Three Essays on Drive and Desire.* London: Karnac.
– Verhaeghe, P. (2009). *New Studies of Old Villains: a Radical Reconsideration of the Oedipus Complex.* New York: Other Press.
– Warlick, M.E. (2001). *Max Ernst and Alchemy.* Austin: University of Texas Press.

Spare Me A Pound – An initial look at the Sui Genericism of Austin and Ezra

Carl Abrahamsson

The human need to create is essentially a central part of the cluster that is usually termed the "survival instinct." If our beloved forefathers and foremothers hadn't been on the forefront of foresight, and developed a trust in their immediate intuitions – and a forceful application of their ensuing impulses – this book that you now hold in your hands would never have existed. Nor our general culture as we know it. We constitute the direct result of a long period of time of constant refinement of the battle against any kind of inertia, because we know instinctively that inertia equals death: the very antithesis of survival.

In our modern and chaotic culture, people still carry traces of this primordial creativity but for the most part it has been relegated to "professionals" – whether that be politicians creating safe environments, the military protecting this specific habitat, or the artists who are trained at prestigious schools to be sensitive in their reflections of what's going on around us.

This compartmentalized institutionalization of survival is neither good nor bad; neither constructive nor destructive. What has happened though, is that the view of creativity as such has been narrowed down to a time- and space-specific activity; and not as an allround extension of an instinct we all actually share. Needless to say, this has diluted the quality and potency of the original function of art: of making people aware of necessary survival mechanisms.

Art should present and represent potential – the very first (and perhaps therefore the most important) game board upon which we evaluate where we should move next. Traditionally, the artist was much more powerful than today. Why? Because the artist had that power of presenting and representing potential. This position of reverence and respect has travelled onwards genetically as well as culturally; often contained within a socio-cultural complex we could describe as "individual survival by outstanding excellence." If our tribe members project respect and awe upon us, our own chances of survival greatly increase. (This exclusive position could of course backfire too, if the presentations and representations of the artist turn out to be erroneous or threatening to the well-being of the tribe itself.)

Talented and creative children should be encouraged to develop their skills and creativity. But even if that's not the case, their need to create and express doesn't go away. It just becomes stronger than any external discouragement. In some milder cases this manifests as honing a skill within the boundaries of a "hobby." That is, a time- and space-relegated ventilation mechanism. In other cases, where the need for acknowledgment is stronger (usually because of active external oppression/repression), the need becomes part of a pathology in which talent and need become united, overheated, and disregarding of conventions and accepted behavioral patterns.

Examples of this would be the "troubled genius" or the "starving artist," whose forceful and sometimes (paradoxically) self-destructive drive to not only create but also to display the creations in question constitutes a shard or a remnant of another facet of the atavistic artist archetype – that of a shaman who goes beyond the senses to bring back information and inspiration from other strata of consciousness – even at the risk of being ridiculed.

When there is a discrepancy between sender and receiver, for instance because of autistically fragranced inabilities or insensitivities within the sender, this only increases the fervor or temperature in an already overheated mind. One way of dealing with this inadequate level of acknowledgement is by adding the dimensions of contextualization and systemization; that is, a meta-level augmenting the great skill one already (supposedly) has. In this way, the original art or signal is repackaged and enhanced through its own contextualized reverberation. These systems can be advanced, elaborate and eloquent to the degree that they eventually even overshadow the original expression or talent. And thus can become new avenues or even career opportunities in the ever developing process of acknowledgement and survival.

Looking at two prominent 20th century creatives – American poet Ezra Pound (1885-1972) and British artist Austin Osman Spare (1886-1956) – we can clearly see this fascinating aspect of the development of added levels of neurosis.

Both gentlemen were prodigious, and developed not only skill and expertise but also a transcendence both in process and expression (meaning, they both engaged so fiercely in their creative process that the rational mind with its many inhibiting forces was set aside – sidetracked or short-circuited – so that irrational and subconscious signals could pass through and into the creative process). Furthermore, they were both highly ambitious and productive; yet not in striving for mainstream acceptance.

They both focussed on refining their tools and languages; their approaches and symbologies; acknowledging the influence of contemporary psychology and its importance, yet striving for a distanced aloofness by attaching themselves to a "classicism," or an aspect of cultural eternity only expressible in a specific art form they felt a strong affinity with.

Pound not only wrote beautiful and mind-expanding poetry and essays. He also early on assumed the position of teacher and authority. This not only by displaying quantitative "objective" knowledge that could be imparted, but mainly through his own insight and systemization being presented as uniquely his own. *ABC of Reading* and *Guide to Kulchur*, for instance, are two book titles prominently displaying a position not only of expertise but of prerogative.

This quasi-hubristic position both helped and hampered Pound when he was confined to St. Elisabeth's mental hospital in Washington, DC, between 1946 and

1958 (following his support for Benito Mussolini's fascist Italy during and after WW2). The defense argued insanity (basically so that Pound would escape a considerably more draconian punishment). It was also apparent that Pound at this time exercised an authority in certain cultural spheres (literary, poetic) but that it was essentially self-sustained over a long period of time.

From teaching curious acolytes at his positively ad-libbing "Ezuversity" in rural Italy during the 1930s, to writing a great number of literary reviews and essays judging the quality of other authors' writings and attitudes, Pound rode the high horse, and that for a reason: the avant garde and supremely talented poet expanded his own assumption of authority as a survival mechanism.

After Pound himself had been judged insane, his main spokesperson and aide Julian Cornell wrote to Pound's wife Dorothy that she "...need not be alarmed about the report on your husband's mental condition... I feel quite sure that you will find, when you see him again, that he is his usual self, and that the mental aberrations which the doctors have found are not anything new or unusual, but are chronic and would pass entirely unnoticed by one like yourself who has lived close to him for a number of years. In fact I think it may be fairly said that any man of his genius would be regarded by a psychiatrist as abnormal."[1]

Austin Osman Spare was a highly skilled draughtsman and painter who received praise for his talents early on. However, instead of pursuing a successful career of portraiture, for instance, Spare spent most of his life in financially dire straits, painting pub punters for small sums and seemingly cherishing his "splendid isolation."

Spare also wrote several books outlining his own perspectives on psychology, sexuality, and magic (of the occult, supernatural kind, for instance in his 1913 magnum opus *The Book of Pleasure (Self Love) – The Psychology of Ecstasy*); often intimately connecting these with his own artistic process. His manic creativity simply wouldn't settle for visual expressions clearly marked by his own artistic genius. There was also an apparent need to contextualize his own creativity and place it on a philosophical and magico-religious level which he and he alone could systematize and assume authority over.

Where Pound was in every way a radical classicist, looking back to antiquity (both eastern and western) and finding solace in his own position as caretaker of a legacy, Spare looked back even further. He argued that through his construction of an "alphabet of desire," it was possible to magically reawaken atavistic layers of the human psyche (for purposes of increased self-knowledge, sexual prowess, power and problem-solving capacities, for instance). Thus acknowledging that we all carry the tangible traces of evolution within us – as displayed physically in the gradual development of a human fetus.

Spare's "atavistic resurgence" could be willed, he argued, by using his "magical alphabet" and creative techniques (such as "automatic" drawing, painting and writing), and by mentally focussing on "sigils" (ideogrammatic symbols of the desired outcome) while in ecstatic mind-frames (such as the orgasm).

---

1 Julian Cornell to Dorothy Pound, quoted in Carpenter, Humphrey, *A Serious Character – The Life of Ezra Pound*, Faber & Faber, London, 1988, p 723.

The potential empowerment of the individual here comes through the position of pupil; a subjugation to the theories and practices of the artistic master magician and psychologically very liberal systematizer-teacher. This was of course exactly the situation at Pound's classes in Italy, too.

Pound often reflected upon the very nature of teaching, and shared his thoughts in works like *ABC of Reading*:

> "The man who really knows can tell all that is transmissible in a very few words. The economic problem of the teacher (of violin or of language or of anything else) is how to string it out so as to be paid for more lessons."[2]

> "Real education must ultimately be limited to men who INSIST on knowing, the rest is mere sheep-herding."[3]

Even this apparently critical attitude towards conventional teaching becomes a telling decoy of sorts, making our attention move from Pound as Poet to Pound as Teacher, and onwards to Pound as Arbiter of Teaching. This abstraction and detachment is clever and often demagogically eloquent, as could be expected from a brilliantly overheated mind like Pound's. But at the same time the intricacy and intelligence in many ways reveal a deep fear of being scrutinized by others.

> "As the press, daily, weekly, and monthly, is utterly corrupted, either from economic or personal causes, it is manifestly UP TO the teaching profession to act for themselves without waiting for the journalists and magazine blokes to assist them. The mental life of a nation is no man's private property. The function of the teaching profession is to maintain the HEALTH OF THE NATIONAL MIND. As there are great specialists and medical discoverers, so there are 'leading writers;' but once a discovery is made, the local practitioner is just as inexcusable as the discoverer himself if he fails to make use of the known remedies and known prophylactics."[4]

The same argument can be made for or about Spare: the detachment in his case is not only simply writing about the tools of his apparent trade in passages about "automatic" drawing and writing. It goes even further when the magical thinking becomes systematized, and he thereby can offer a perspective on not only changing himself but also others. It's another level of attractive distancing; a glamor spell of sorts:

> "The Ego is desire, so everything is ultimately desired and undesirable, desire is ever a preliminary forecast of terrible dissatisfaction hidden

2 Pound, Ezra, *ABC of Reading*, Faber & Faber, London, 1991, p 83.

3 Ibid, p 84.

4 Pound, Ezra, "The Teacher's Mission," in *Literary Essays of Ezra Pound*, New Directions, New York, 1968, p 59.

> by its ever-present vainglory. The millennium will come and quickly go. Men will be greater than the Gods they ever conceived – there will be greater dissatisfaction. You are ever what you were – but you may be so in a different form!"[5]

What is the hubristic hen here, and what is the ensouled egg of excellence? I would argue that the "passion of immersion" in talents like Pound and Spare, both definitely touched by genius, can create psychic overheating in the human mind, which then needs to be justified in regard to the outside world – so as not to be discounted as belonging to someone "crazy."

Both gentlemen to a great extent discarded the outer in order to refine the inner. But as that, for distinctly neurotic reasons, apparently wasn't enough, they both added the dimension of systemization, and thereby assumed a constructed authority.

Spare self-published his books and had occasional exhibitions of his art. Pound's books were published and were definitely well-respected, mainly within an environment of modernist letters. As both men had this kind of external agency, we cannot claim that their assuming of authority was purely compensational (as in cases in which neurotics or psychotics create manically in more or less total isolation because they have no other choice).

I would argue that it's here more a case of *Sui Genericism* (the amplification of one's own sense of greatness through systemized interpretation and dissemination): it is not a case of hubris pure and simple; nor of narcissism per se; nor of a fascistoid character type (à la Fromm) demanding "followers."

The extra dimension of systemization never took away from their core need: to express themselves in a unique, creative way. The systemization was rather an accumulating reinforcement via shared monologues that eventually crystallized and became real, solid legacies: Spare's books are kept in print and written about, mainly in the world of contemporary occultism, and Pound is revered as an inspiring and educating classicist mind as much as an introspective and groundbreaking poet. They may have been in a league of their own – genuine "Sui Generis" individuals – but their own reinforcements are equally valid keys to understanding their legacy in general, as well as inspiring spring boards for new generations of acolytes.

It is interesting to note that both gentlemen were quite critical of psychology, and of the gradual acceptance of this relatively new science in the mainstream culture. Spare called Freud and Jung "Fraud" and "Junk" but according to his friend, disciple and biographer, Kenneth Grant, Spare apparently "sent a copy of *The Book of Pleasure* to Sigmund Freud who described it as one of the most significant revelations of subconscious mechanisms that had appeared in modern times."[6] If this actually happened (as yet unconfirmed!) it would surely have made Spare supremely happy in his own *Sui Genericism*. The ultimately desired is always external acknowledgment.

Pound was less ambiguous in his views of Freud, calling his teaching, "unmitigat-

5 Spare, Austin Osman, *The Book of Pleasure (Self-Love) – The Psychology of Ecstasy,* 93 Publishing, Canada, 1975, p 26.

6 Grant, Kenneth, "Introduction" in Spare, Austin Osman, *The Book of Pleasure (Self-Love) – The Psychology of Ecstasy*, 93 Publishing, Canada, 1975, p VIII.

ed shit... laid out in most elegant arabesques."[7] Pound's general hatred of psychology also got meshed with his blatant antisemitism: "the Vienese poison... whole pewk of kiketry, aimed at destroying the will / introspective idiocy / non objective."[8] Whether this was a shield of defense against the potential scrutiny of any critical nay-sayers or just a Poundful of elegant arabesques enforcing the position of the poet-classicist as untouchable master, the main insight remains the same: the intellectual movements of Pound's time to a very great extent embraced Freud's theories on sexuality and the unconscious, and also lauded Freud himself as a "prophet" of sorts. Although Pound was interested in many of the same Zeitgeist topics, he could never deflate himself to not be the main casual "expounder" of wisdom in his own particularly fragmented style, and just accept someone else's formulations of the same insights – especially if those formulations were coming from a Jew!

For many creatives, the time and space to concentrate and let ideas flow unhampered is absolutely essential – in the case of neurotics and psychotics these prerequisites can even seem to be vital. No wonder then, that isolation was a key element for both Spare and Pound. Pound's "expatriotism" was established already in 1908, when he first moved to London. From then and on he stayed away from the US as much as he could. This willed expatriate isolation greatly helped him immerse himself in studies and creative writing. In no way a total introspective, Pound's estrangement from American culture seems to have been one of preference and cultural inspiration rather than anything else.

Pound's stay at St. Elisabeth's Hospital between 1946 and 1958 was also an isolation, but certainly an unwanted one. Pound could read, write and see friends and family members, but the stay actually brought with it exactly the mental imbalance that he was there to be "cured" of.

Spare's isolation, on the other hand, was always wholly self-imposed. He retracted to his inner spheres and brought out fantastic vistas to paint; apparently transcending time and space, Spare seems to have been needing peace and quiet. As he had already been subjected to some degree of fame early on in life, he certainly knew what he was missing. His own artistic and occult experiments simply seemed more important. I suspect that an extroversion in terms of nurturing a career would also have meant an increased sense of dreaded scrutiny and criticism. I believe Spare felt safe and optimally creative in his own self-imposed poverty. Spare's *Sui Genericism* needed to be controlled and directed by himself, and not be exposed to the potential threats of outer criticism.

There are other similarities beyond parallel existences in time, basic psychological constitutions and using far off, distant times as romantic escapisms. Both men integrated an ideogrammatic method for reaching communicatory clarity. Pound's interest in, and occasionally obsession with, Chinese characters of writing was a part of a strong, seemingly pathological drive to join the dots within poetic expression for it to bloom into a "total" expression beyond the "normal."

The desire to break down elements, phenomena and even the psyche into the

---

7 Carpenter, Humphrey, *A Serious Character – The Life of Ezra Pound*, Faber & Faber, London, 1988, p 395.

8 Ibid, p 395.

smallest possible unit was undoubtedly a Zeitgeist phenomenon. The early 20th century development of atomic research for purposes of energy and eventually warfare suddenly transcended history, as it grew out of Greek antiquity by association with the very word. The original Greek word Atomos means "indivisible," signifying the smallest possible building block. As the scientists of Spare and Pound's day were looking for a way of harnessing the huge amounts of energy stemming from either fission or fusion, so were the radical poets and artists; and so were the pioneering psychologists and psychoanalysts. Breaking down something inherently meant laying it bare, and as such it could be evaluated and then reassembled in desired ways.

For Spare, the literal stripping of conventional meaning from a word by not only decimation of superfluous characters but then also by reshaping the remaining ones into an ideogram meant to be immediately forgotten, post-ecstatic experience, became a central part of his "teaching" and system. Weaving these new and "sentient" symbols into his mind via "automatic" images and writings became an even greater artwork in itself: a psychic *Gesamtkunstwerk* that he was the creator of.

For Pound, the main power of language, and of poetry specifically, was the evocative potential of bringing forth images in the mind. His reverence for the Chinese characters, which have developed from pictograms to ideograms over time, became a tool in his own poetic creation – as did the entire specifically Confucian philosophy. Making no distinction between times, spaces and cultures, Pound pragmatically brought the small evocative units into his own machinery of leverage. For instance, by "translating" and editing the beloved *Shih-Ching* (the classic anthology of Chinese odes defined by Confucius), Pound was basically also writing his own book.

> "No one is going to be content with a transliteration of Chinese names. When not making a desperate effort at mnemonics or differentiating in vain hope of distinguishing one race from another, I mainly use the French form. Our European knowledge of China has come via Latin and French and at any rate the French novels as printed have some sort of uniform connotation."[9]

Pound's frequent integration of the actual Chinese characters throughout his masterpiece Cantos (along with Greek and Egyptian hieroglyphs) is not solely an attempt at being clever but a way of creating an intellectual assault that leads to an emotional-psychic release in the immersion of the images evoked. What has made Pound one of the most respected poets of the 20th century is exactly this audacity: taking whatever sources that inspire you and using an uninhibited artistic and poetic license to refine and define them.

For Pound, the admiration for – and perhaps identification with – the Chinese philosopher Confucius is essential to understanding his psychic constitution. Pound looked beyond time and space, assumed authority (again) by translating/formulating Confucius, and thereby brought someone else's thoughts and language under his own umbrella of definition. This is evident in the strictly philosophical perspective as

9 Pound, Ezra, *The Cantos of Ezra Pound*, New Directions, New York, 1993, p 254.

well: Pound demagogically challenged the status quo of western academia by placing himself in this role as interpreter. We can see a similar occurrence in Pound's critique of contemporary financial systems: his was a genuine interest in alternative currencies and financial methods (like, taxation only of financial sectors but not of sectors of manufacture) but the potentially constructive demagogia was hampered (to say the least) by Pound's vocal adherence to an antisemitic prejudice that permeated a lot of his thinking.

According to Pound's son-in-law, the Italian anthropologist Boris de Rachewiltz, he was "...constantly at work breaking down outworn symbols into their original components, once more restoring them to some of their earlier power by making them new. This is, after all, quite an appropriate function for a poet in his role as a perpetuator of traditions temporarily lost from sight."[10]

For Spare, the development of his "alphabet of desire" had proto- or meta-creative potential. He presented his method in *The Book Of Pleasure* and other texts; outlining his core idea that it's not so much his esthetic approach that is the key but a wholly individual one. Basically: anyone could use the method, regardless of artistic skills. By stripping down superfluous letters in a word or a sentence expressing the desired, for instance, one then takes the remaining unique letters and recomposes them into a graphic glyph that is no longer discernible as "rational" writing. This glyph is then, according to Spare's schematic magical view, "dropped" into the subconscious during an ecstatic mind-frame, and from which it blooms as a desired manifestation of events. A traditional, rational smallest common (/communion) denominator is reshaped by will into an ideogrammatic unit to be integrated in a magical worldview – disseminated by the master magician, of course.

Reconstructing proto-letters via unique expertise is an important part of their respective defense mechanisms. Both wanted to strip down the norm and chisel out an innermost meaning that could then be put to new poetic-magical use in their own systems. Both wanted to expound a new meaning and then spare (pardon the puns!) the mind the inert machinations of the normal/rational. And both used their creative geniuses as the main constructive agents or tools. The times couldn't have been more perfect for artistic experiments like this, and I believe that the Zeitgeist itself was more instrumental for them both than they cared to admit.

In many ways, Spare was the quintessential surrealist in both form and content, ever experimenting with both, as well as acknowledging psychology and the subconscious as a very real and useful sphere. Pound was as affected by the First World War as everyone else, and actively sought out a constructive contrarian position in modernist letters as student-teacher-editor-reviewer, and then as an ambitious Poet Laureate of a disgruntled post-WW1-world seeking new meanings and new forms.

Through their brilliance, they also helped (re)shape their times. Pound more immediately so, as he actually made an impact during his own lifetime. Spare had to wait a few decades after his death in 1956 before real, outer acknowledgement took place; mainly thanks to occult-related people rather than an art world as such. Strate-

10 de Rachewiltz, Boris, "Pagan and Magic Elements," in Hesse, Eva (ed), *New Approaches to Ezra Pound*, University of California Press, Berkeley & Los Angeles, 1969, p 195.

gic mentions by key people like Kenneth Grant, Genesis P-Orridge, Jimmy Page, the Atlantis Bookshop in London, and the publishing company Fulgur have made Spare a thoroughly revived British treasure, and one whose respect is now also reflected in the art market's increasing prices of his works.

There is another very interesting trait that unites these two men and their quite unique psychic composites, and we could literally call it a "seminal" one. Spare's active use of the vacuity or psychic void at the moment of orgasm (or other ecstatic experiences) was a central part of the ritual aspects of his teachings. Being an avid masturbator helped his creativity reach new heights, he claimed, and he also used local women and prostitutes in the poorer areas of London where he lived. To Spare, it didn't matter if these women were beautiful or traditionally "arousing." For him, these sexual partners were merely vehicles and vessels for him to charge his magical "sigils" during orgasms, and to induce post-orgasmic trances during which he saw subconscious vistas and landscapes that he then recreated in stunningly eerie and beautiful images.

> "The conception is the absence of its indisputable reality or reality within! when the conception is memorial to forgetfulness – it may be the chance of its reality for you? when the prayer – (you are always praying) has transmitted to its blasphemy – you are attractive enough to be heard – your desire is gratified! What a somersault of humility!"[11]

> "Ideas of Self in conflict cannot be slain, by resistance they are a reality – no Death or cunning has overcome them but is their reinforcement of energy. The dead are born again and again lie in the womb of conscience. By allowing maturity is to predicate decay – when by non-resistance is retrogression to early simplicity and the passage to the original and unity without the idea. From that idea is the formula of non-resistance germinating. 'Does not matter – please yourself.'"[12]

Pound's perspective was equally out of the ordinary. Highly inspired by the French author Remy de Gourmont (1858-1915, whose writings Pound also translated – probably more correctly than those of Confucius), Pound claimed that the orgasm, and the semen specifically, sets free aspects of genius that otherwise remain passive.

> "... it is more than likely that the brain itself is, in origin and development, only a sort of great clot of genital fluid held in suspense or reserve..."[13]

> "The spermatozoid is, I take it, regarded as a sort of quintessence, or

11 Spare, Austin Osman, *The Book of Pleasure (Self-Love) – The Psychology of Ecstasy*, 93 Publishing, Canada, 1975, p 13.

12 Ibid, p 17.

13 Pound, Ezra, "Translator's Postscript", in de Gourmont, Remy, *The Natural Philosophy of Love*, Rarity Press, New York, 1931, p 169.

> at least 'in rapport with' all parts of the body; the single spermatozoid demands simply that the ovule shall construct a human being, the suspended spermatozoid (if my wild shot rings the target bell) is ready to dispense with, in the literal sense, incarnation, en-fleshment. Shall we postulate the mass of spermatozoids, first accumulated in suspense, then specialized?"[14]

In our view of these gentlemen as supremely creative but also over-heated, leading to the necessary defense mechanism of Sui Genericism, this ultimate, creative perspective fits as well. Taking on the role of someone who is not only a master of their overall individual creative aspects – their "tools of the trade" – but also the role of the divulger of mysteries pertaining to one of the most absolute and attractive core essences of human preoccupation (and life) – sex! – they write and paint themselves into a desired position of mastery. And they succeeded, albeit to varying degrees.

In the contemporary art world, Spare is lauded as an underestimated British genius, and the prices of drawings and paintings are constantly increasing. His occultism is well-respected and never overtly criticized or questioned. New studies, biographies, and occasional exhibitions feed an increased interest in this quirky character that obviously had something going for him.

Pound was confined to a mental hospital for 12 years, which understandably broke down his general sense of *joie de vivre*, and yet he retained his ideas, positions and his creativity upon returning to his beloved Italy, albeit in a more fragmented output.

To say that these specific creatives were "outsider" artists is not correct. Both of them exist in the real, "acknowledged" world of their respective expressions, and they certainly do so by their own design and agency. Thus, if any outsider-isms are to be taken into account, they exist by willed positioning rather than, as is more traditionally accepted when we consider the term, as an attempt of making virtues out of necessities. Many "outsider" artists lack the agency to be on the inside, and therefore take pride in their position rather than try to overcome it.

There are many art historians and theoreticians who argue that the so-called outsider art is a more genuine form of art, as it is more clearly related to the origins of art and its functions thanks to the pure pathology of the artist. Here we could consider Spare and Pound as existing in a grey area in-between "outsiders" and "insiders." Fervently seeking acknowledgement for their brilliance by developing *Sui Genericism*, they never compromised their essential sense of integrity, nor the quality of their output. But at the same time they did undeniably invite extra praise via complex structures of supra-agency.

Perhaps we could even conclude by stating that their respective magics actually seem to have worked very well indeed?

---

14 Ibid, p 178.

> "Art is the instinctive application (to observations or sensations) of the knowledge latent in the sub-consciousness."[15]

References

– Carpenter, Humphrey, *A Serious Character – The Life of Ezra Pound*, Faber & Faber, London, 1988.
– De Gourmont, Remy, *The Natural Philosophy of Love*, Rarity Press, New York, 1931.
– Hesse, Eva (ed), *New Approaches to Ezra Pound*, University of California Press, Berkeley & Los Angeles, 1969.
– Pound, Ezra, *ABC of Reading*, Faber & Faber, London, 1991.
– Pound, Ezra, *The Cantos of Ezra Pound*, New Directions, New York, 1993.
– Pound, Ezra, *Literary Essays of Ezra Pound*, New Directions, New York, 1968.
– Spare, Austin Osman, *The Book of Pleasure (Self-Love) – The Psychology of Ecstasy*, 93 Publishing, Canada, 1975.

15 Spare, Austin Osman, *The Book of Pleasure (Self-Love) – The Psychology of Ecstasy*, 93 Publishing, Canada, 1975, p 55.

Contributors

Carl Abrahamsson is a Swedish author based in Stockholm. Since the mid-1980s he has explored underground culture of many kinds; predominantly what is nowadays termed "occulture." His books include *Different People* (2021), *The Devil's Footprint* (2020), *Occulture* (2018), *Reasonances* (2014), *Mother, Have A Safe Trip* (2013) and many others. He is also the editor and publisher of the eclectic journal of magico-anthropology: *The Fenris Wolf.*
www.carlabrahamsson.com www.patreon.com/vanessa23carl

Val Denham (b. 1957) is an artist, poet, musician and transgender icon. She has been creating her own universe since being a little boy. Val received her formal training at Bradford College and The Royal College of Art, London from 1974 to 1982. She has been described as "one of the greatest colourists" by abstract artist Patrick Heron, a visiting tutor at the Royal College of Art. Her art explores her own inner workings and the transformations she has gone through. She is also an accomplished portrait artist. She has been labelled an outsider artist in some quarters, however, she describes herself as a cleaning lady. Val perfectly explains her modus operandi: "I employ both a figurative and non-figurative abstract semi surrealist symbolism… my art is a kind of therapy… the internal map of my neuroses, severe Obsessive Compulsive Disorder and gender dysphoria… analyse the surface of Tranart (Val's name for her own art) and you will glimpse neurotic hieroglyphs trying to describe what it is to be me… meanings are always masked in a kind of visual code within my work. Even now I employ obscuring patterns and imagery; though the reason to do so no longer exists… I no longer live a double life suppressing my true nature, but the code remains." She releases her own idiosyncratic songs on both official record labels and her own unofficial Invisible Vagina label. She has an ever growing fan base across the world.

Inez Edström is an artist and nurse, who directs the art studio at the Psychiatric clinic at Östra Sjukhuset, Gothenburg.

Per Magnus Johansson is a psychoanalyst trained in Paris. He is a licensed psychologist, PhD and Associate professor in the History of Ideas at the University of Gothenburg (GU). He teaches psychoanalytic theory, psychoanalytic psychotherapy and Foucauldian discourse analysis, and many other topics. He is also in private practice in Gothenburg. His research mainly concerns the history of psychoanalysis, psychotherapy and psychiatry.

Christian Munthe is professor of practical philosophy at the University of Gothenburg. His research targets the ethics of health policy and healthcare in a broad sense. One of his concentrations has been the area of mental health and psychiatry, among other things in the Centre for Ethics, Law and Mental Health (CELAM).

Johannes Nordholm is a psychologist, coordinator at the General Psychiatry Clinic at Sahlgrenska University Hospital, art educator at the Gothenburg Museum of Art, art writer and member of the editorial board of the Gothenburg-based cultural journal *Arche.*

Elisabeth Punzi is a licensed psychologist, PhD and Associate professor of psychology at the Department of Social work, University of Gothenburg. She writes about the history of psychoanalysis and its Jewish heritage. Her research concerns the meaning of creative activities and how the unique client and his/hers experiences and context might be the starting point for research as well as clinical practice. She mainly writes from critical perspectives. She also works with the Center for Critical Heritage Studies, University of Gothenburg, where she directs the work on heritage and health, with a specific interest in the heritage of psychiatry and Mad people's history/heritage.

Vanessa Sinclair, Psy.D. is a psychoanalyst who relocated from New York City to Stockholm and sees clients internationally. She is the author of *Scansion in Psychoanalysis and Art: the Cut in Creation* (Routledge, 2020) and *Switching Mirrors* (Trapart Books, 2016); editor of *Rendering Unconscious: Psychoanalytic Perspectives, Politics & Poetry* (Trapart Books, 2019); co-editor of *On Psychoanalysis and Violence: Contemporary Lacanian Perspectives* (Routledge, 2018) with Manya Steinkoler and *The Fenris Wolf*, vol. 9 (Trapart Books, 2017) with Carl Abrahamsson. Dr. Sinclair hosts the Rendering Unconscious podcast, addressing the state of psychoanalysis and mental health care, politics, the arts, culture and current events. She is a founding member of Das Unbehagen: A Free Association for Psychoanalysis, and arranges psychoanalytic conferences internationally. For more information, please visit:
www.drvanessasinclair.net www.patreon.com/vanessa23carl

ALSO AVAILABLE FROM TRAPART BOOKS

Vanessa Sinclair (Ed.):
Rendering Unconscious – Psychoanalytic Perspectives, Politics & Poetry

In times of crisis, one needs to stop and ask, "How did we get here?" Our contemporary chaos is the result of a society built upon pervasive systems of oppression, discrimination and violence that run deeper and reach further than most understand or care to realize. These draconian systems have been fundamental to many aspects of our lives, and we seem to have gradually allowed them more power. However, our foundation is not solid; it is fractured and collapsing – if we allow that. We need to start applying new models of interpretation and analysis to the deep-rooted problems at hand.

Rendering Unconscious brings together international scholars, psychoanalysts, psychologists, philosophers, researchers, writers and poets; reflecting on current events, politics, the state of mental health care, the arts, literature, mythology, and the cultural climate; thoughtfully evaluating this moment of crisis, its implications, wide-ranging effects, and the social structures that have brought us to this point of urgency.

Hate speech, Internet stalking, virtual violence, the horde mentality of the alt-right, systematic racism, the psychology of rioting, the theater of violence, fake news, the power of disability, erotic transference and counter-transference, the economics of libido, Eros and the death drive, fascist narratives, psychoanalytic formation as resistance, surrealism and sexuality, traversing genders, and colonial counterviolence are but a few of the topics addressed in this thought-provoking and inspiring volume.

Contributions by Vanessa Sinclair, Gavriel Reisner, Alison Annunziata, Kendalle Aubra, Gerald Sand, Tanya White-Davis & Anu Kotay, Luce deLire, Jason Haaf, Simon Critchley & Brad Evans, Marc Strauss, Chiara Bottici, Manya Steinkoler, Emma Lieber, Damien Patrick Williams, Shara Hardeson, Jill Gentile, Angelo Villa, Gabriela Costardi, Jamieson Webster, Sergio Benvenuto, Craig Slee, Álvaro D. Moreira, David Lichtenstein, Julie Fotheringham, John Dall'aglio, Matthew Oyer, Jessica Datema, Olga Cox Cameron, Katie Ebbitt, Juliana Portilho, Trevor Pederson, Elisabeth Punzi & Per-Magnus Johansson, Meredith Friedson, Steven Reisner, Léa Silveira, Patrick Scanlon, Júlio Mendes Rodrigo, Daniel Deweese, Julie Futrell, Gregory J. Stevens, Benjamin Y. Fong, Katy Bohinc, Wayne Wapeemukwa, Patricia Gherovici & Cassandra Seltman, Marie Brown, Buffy Cain, Claire-Madeline Culkin, Andrew Daul, Germ Lynn, Adel Souto, and paul aster stone-tsao.

Vanessa Sinclair: *Switching Mirrors*

Switching Mirrors is an amazing collection of cut-ups and mind-expanding poetry by Vanessa Sinclair. Delving into the unconscious and actively utilising the "third mind" as developed by William S Burroughs and Brion Gysin, Sinclair roams through suggestive vistas of magic, witchcraft, dreams, psychoanalysis, sex and sexuality (and more). Causal apprehensions are disrupted by a flow of impressions that open up the mind of the reader. What's behind language and our use of it? What happens when random factors and the unconscious are given free reign in poetic form? Switching Mirrors is what happens.

Genesis Breyer P-Orridge:
Sacred Intent - Conversations with Carl Abrahamsson 1986-2019

Sacred Intent gathers conversations between artist Genesis Breyer P-Orridge and longtime friend and collaborator, the Swedish author Carl Abrahamsson. From the first 1986 fanzine interview about current projects, over philosophical insights, magical workings, international travels, art theory and gender revolutions, to 2019's thoughts on life and death in the the shadow of battling leukaemia, Sacred Intent is a unique journey in which the art of conversation blooms.

With (in)famous projects like C.O.U.M. Transmissions, Throbbing Gristle, Psychic TV, Thee Temple Ov Psychick Youth (TOPY) and Pandrogeny, Breyer P-Orridge has consistently thwarted preconceived ideas and transformed disciplines such as performance art, music, collage, poetry and social criticism; always cutting up the building blocks to dismantle control structures and authority. But underneath the socially conscious and pathologically rebellious spirit, there has always been a devout respect for a holistic, spiritual, magical worldview - one of "sacred intent."

Sacred Intent is a must read for anyone interested in contemporary art, deconstructed identity, gender evolution, and magical philosophy. The book not only celebrates an intimate friendship, but also the work and ideas of an artist who has never ceased to amaze and provoke. Also included are photographic portraits of Breyer P-Orridge taken by Carl Abrahamsson, transcripts of key lectures, and an interview with Jacqueline "Lady Jaye" Breyer P-Orridge from 2004.

Genesis Breyer P-Orridge: *Brion Gysin - His Name Was Master*

Brion Gysin (1916–86) has been an incredibly influential artist and iconoclast: his development of the "cut-up" technique with William S. Burroughs has inspired generations of writers, artists and musicians. Gysin was also a skilled networker and revered expat: together with his friend Paul Bowles, he more or less constructed the post-beatnik romanticism for life and magic in Morocco, and was also a protagonist in an international gay culture with inspirational reaches in both America and Europe. Not surprisingly, Gysin has become something of a cult figure.

One of the artists he inspired is Genesis Breyer P-Orridge, who collaborated with both Gysin and Burroughs in the 1970s, during his work with Throbbing Gristle and C.O.U.M. Transmissions. The interviews made by P-Orridge have since become part of a New Wave/ Industrial mythos. This volume presents them in their entirety alongside three texts on Gysin by P-Orridge, plus an introduction. This book is an exclusive insight into the mind of a man P-Orridge describes as "a kind of Leonardo da Vinci of the last century," and a fantastic complement to existing biographies and monographs.

Carl Abrahamsson: *Genesis P-Orridge:*
Temporarily Eternal - Photographs 1986-2018

Temporarily Eternal is an emotional-visual summing up of a creative friendship between Swedish author Carl Abrahamsson and British artist Genesis P-Orridge (1950-2020) that lasted for more than three decades, and which was filled with musical projects, films, books, writings, conversations, travel, and a great deal of magic. This book both is and is not a companion to Genesis Breyer P-Orridge: Sacred Intent - Conversations with Carl Abrahamsson 1986-2019. It is, in the sense that the present book also focuses on shared moments during the same period of time. It is not, in the sense that it's not an intellectual trip into concepts and thoughts expressed via language, in conversation. Instead, this book contains photographic portraits: some are staged, considered, thought through, and some are pure snapshots of auspicious and fleeting moments. And some are definitely somewhere in between: juggling immediate form with desired content.

Carl Abrahamsson: *Different People*

"Different People" is an anthology of interviews by Swedish author Carl Abrahamsson, focusing on art, life and the creative process. Included are in-depth conversations with Conrad Rooks, Malcolm McLaren, Stelarc, John Duncan, Charles Gatewood, Mark McCloud, Ralph Metzner, Peter Beard, Bill Landis, Ralph Gibson, Maja Elliott, Michael Bowen, Bob Colacello, Dian Hanson, Anton Corbijn, June Newton, Kendell Geers, Simeon Coxe III (Silver Apples), Vicki Bennett (People Like Us), and Brian Williams (Lustmord). These groundbreaking artists, writers, musicians, photographers, filmmakers, editors and psychedelic researchers have all helped shape the culture we live in. But what makes them do what they do? Which are their driving forces and their inspirations; their joys and fears?

Carl Abrahamsson: *The Devil's Footprint*

God proposes the challenge of the millennium: if Satan sorts out the ever growing human mess on Earth, God will lovingly take him back to Heaven as his favorite Archangel. Satan accepts, and sets out on a massive operation to balance out over-population, pollution, corruption, and other severely Satanic headaches – many of which he originally helped create... Easier said than done! Satan's love of the ambitiously mischievous humans is challenged as his own "Team Apocalypse" fervently sets to work. But as the world begins to change quickly and dramatically for the better, a new question arises: can God and his suspicious Archangels really be trusted in this cataclysmic, cosmic undertaking?

Carl Abrahamsson: *Mother, Have A Safe Trip*

Unearthed plans and designs stemming from radical inventor Nikola Tesla could solve the world's energy problems. These plans suddenly generate a vortex of interest from various powers. Thrown into this maelstrom of international intrigue is Victor Ritterstadt – a soul searching magician with a mysterious and troubled past. From Berlin, over Macedonia, and all the way to Nepal, Ritterstadt sets out on an outer as well as inner quest. Espionage, love, UFOs, magic, telepathy, conspiracies, LSD, and more in this shocking story of a world about to be changed forever…

"It's a thrilling roller coaster ride through psychedelic adventures, juicy romantic interludes, metaphoric dreamscapes, high Himalayan yoga enclaves, telepathic portals, 60's flashbacks, magical constructs, secret government pursuits and many more twists that kept all three of my eyes open. It's a story that you'll definitely want to keep non-stop reading, which I enthusiastically recommend."

– George Douvris, Links by George

"Mother, Have A Safe Trip is a highly entertaining and thought-provoking novel. Chock-full of psychedelia, the book is also a much welcome addition to the far too few fictional works published dealing with psychedelic culture."

– Henrik Dahl, Psychedelic Press

Outsider Inpatient

"The dialogues are great. But it's too short. I wanted more."
– Genesis Breyer P-Orridge, Artist

"It's a wonderful read. A lovely book."
– June Newton/Alice Springs, Photographer

Carl Abrahamsson (Ed.): *The Mega Golem: A Womanual For All Times and Spaces*

An anthology of texts and images constituting the current Corpus of the Mega Golem – the talismanic being/sentience created by Carl Abrahamsson in 2009. With contributions by Carl Abrahamsson, Vanessa Sinclair, Kadmus, Gabriel McCaughry, and others.

***The Fenris Wolf 10* (2020)**

Carl Abrahamsson – Editor's Introduction, Carl Abrahamsson – Onwards to the Source!, Ludwig Klages – On the Essence of Ecstasy, David Beth – Katabasis and Erotognosis, Henrik Dahl – An Introduction to Eroto-Psychedelic Art, Peter Sjöstedt-H – Antichrist Psychonaut: Nietzsche's Psychoactive Drugs, Carl Abrahamsson – Lux Per Nox – The Fenris Wolf As Libidinal Liberator, Jesse Bransford & Max Razdow – Revisiting the Veil of Dreams, Christopher Webster – Beyond the North Wind, Kendell Geers – A Long Boundless Systematized..., Kadmus – Seeking the Three-Headed Saint, Billie Steigerwald – The Chthonic Seed: Reflections of an Ancient Death Gnosis, Fred Andersson – The Gospel According to the Tomb Man, Zaheer Gulamhusein – Sunflower, Charlotte Rodgers – The Riderless Horse..., Craig Slee – The Occult Nature of Cripkult, Damien Patrick Williams – Daoism, Buddhism and Machine Consciousness, Philip H. Farber – Thoughts on the Creation of Memetic Entities, Thomas Bey William Bailey – Memetic Magick, Mitch Horowitz – Is Your Mind a Technology for Utopia?, Ramsey Dukes – I'm Gonna Blow Your Mind, Carl Abrahamsson – Grasping Reality with Gary Lachman, Anders Lundgren – Mike Mignola and the Lovecraft Circle, Peggy Nadramia – So It Was Written, Peggy Nadramia – Addendum to So It Was Written, Nina Antonia – Maya, Jack Stevenson – Häxan/Witchcraft Through the Ages, Andrea Kundry – The Demonic Cultural Legacy of Antonin Artaud, Joan Pope – The Birth of Ideas, Genesis Breyer P-Orridge – Idiosyncratic Use Ov Language..., Vanessa Sinclair – Try To Altar Everything, Claire-Madeline Corso – Cutting Up a New Conversation

***The Fenris Wolf 9* (2017)**

Vanessa Sinclair & Carl Abrahamsson – Editors' Introduction: Looking back at the crossroads, Katelan Foisy – Invocation: Homage to the spirits of the land/London, Sharron Kraus – Art as Alchemy, Demetrius Lacroix – The Seven Layers of the Vodou Soul, Graham Duff – Sublime Fragments: The Art of John Balance, Ken Henson – The American Occult Revival In My Work, Gary Lachman – Was Freud Afraid of the Occult?, Peter Grey – Fly the Light, Val Denham – Proclaim Present Time Over, Katelan Foisy & Vanessa Sinclair – The Cut In Creation, Claire-Madeline Culkin – Beds, Bodies and Other Books of Common Prayer – A Reading of the, Photography of Nan Goldin, Steven Reisner – On the Dance of the Occult and Unconscious in Freud, Katy Bohinc – The 12th House: Art and the Unconscious, Olga Cox Cameron – When Shall We 3 Meet Again? Psychoanalysis, Art and the Occult: A Clandestine Convergence, Ingo Lambrecht – Wairua: Following shamanic contours in psychoanalytic therapy at a Māori Mental Health Service in New Zealand, Elliott Edge – An Occult Reading of PAO! Imagining in the Dark with Our Vestigial Shamanism in a Shade, Shadow, Wide,

Charlotte Rodgers – Stripped to the Core: Animistic Art Action and Magickal Revelation, Alkistis Dimech – Dynamics of the Occulted Body, Fred Yee – Cut-Up As Egregore, Oracle and Flirtation Device, Robert Ansell – Androgyny, Biology and Latent Memory in the Work of Austin Osman Spare, Ray O Neill – Double, Double, Toil and Trouble: Psychoanalysis Burn and Surrealism Bubble, Derek M Elmore – Dreams and the Neither-Neither, Julio Mendes Rodrigo – Rebis, the Double Being, Eve Watson – Bowie's Non-Human Effect: Alien/ Alienation in The Man Who Fell to Earth (1976) and The Hunger (1983), Carl Abrahamsson – Formulating the Desired: Some similarities between ritual magic and the psychoanalytic process

The Fenris Wolf 8 (2016)

Carl Abrahamsson – Editor's Introduction, Vanessa Sinclair – Polymorphous Perversity and Pandrogeny, Charles Stansfield Jones (Frater Achad) – Alchymia, Tim O'Neill: Black Lodge/ White Lodge, Nina Antonia – Bosie & The Beast, Aki Cederberg – Festivals of Spring, Michael Moynihan – Friedrich Hielscher's Vision of the Real Powers, Friedrich Hielscher – The Real Powers, Orryelle Defenestrate Bascule – Ear Horn: Shamanic Perspectives and Multi-Sensory Inversion, Zbigniew Lagos – The Figure of the Polish Magician: Czesław Czynski (1858-1932), Gary Lachman – Rejected Knowledge: A Look At Our Other Way of Knowing, Carl Abrahamsson – Intuition as a State of Grace, Bishop T Omphalos – The Golden Thread: Soteriological Aspects of the Gnostic Catholicism in E.G.C., Kendell Geers – iMagus, Johan Nilsson – Defending Paper Gods: Aleister Crowley and the Reception of Daoism in Early 20th Century Esotericism, Gordan Djurdjevic – The Birth of the New Aeon: Magick and Mysticism of Thelema from the Perspective of Postmodern A/Theology, Tim O'Neill – The Derleth Error, Antti P Balk – Greek Mysteries, Carl Abrahamsson – The Economy of Magic, Stephen Sennitt – The Book of the Sentient Night: 23 Nails, Henrik Dahl – We Ate the Acid: A Note on Psychedelic Imagery, Jason Louv – Robert Anton Wilson's Cosmic Trigger and the Psychedelic Interstellar Future we need, Carey Hodges & Chad Hensley – New Orleans Voodoo: An Oddity Unto Itself, Alexander Nym – Kabbalah references in contemporary culture, Zaheer Gulamhusein – Standing in Line, Carl Abrahamsson – As the Wolf Lies Down to Rest, Vanessa Sinclair & Ingo Lambrecht – Ritual and Psychoanalytical Spaces as Transitional, featuring Sangoma Trance States, Hagen von Julien – Listening to the Voice of Silence: A Contemporary Perspective on the Fraternities Saturni, Erik Davis – Infectious Hoax: Robert Anton Wilson reads H.P. Lovecraft, N – II. Land, Cadmus – Neo-Chthonia, Kadmus – A Fragment of Heart: A contribution to the Mega-Golem, Stojan Nikolic – The One True Church of the Dark Age of Scientism, Miguel Marques – The Labors of Seeing: A Journey Through the Works of Peter Whitehead, Renata Wieczorek – The Conception of Number According to Aleister Crowley, Orryelle Defenestrate Bascule – Fragments of Fact, Derek Seagrief – Conscious ExIt, Kasper Opstrup – By This, That: A spin on Lea Porsager's Spin, and Genesis Breyer P-Orridge – Greyhounds of the future.

The Fenris Wolf 7 (2014)

Carl Abrahamsson – Editor's Introduction, Sara George & Carl Abrahamsson – Fernand Khnopff, Symbolist, Sasha Chaitow – Making the Invisible Visible, Vanessa Sinclair – Psychoanalysis and Dada, Kendell Geers – Tu Marcellus Eris, Stephen Sennitt – Fallen Worlds, Without Shadows, Antony Hequet – Slam Poetry: The Warrior Poet, Antony Hequet – Slam Poetry: The Rebel Poet, Genesis Breyer P-Orridge – Alien Lightning Meat Machine, Genesis Breyer P-Orridge – This Is A Nice Planet, Patrick Lundborg – Psychedelic Philosophy, Henrik

Dahl – Visionary Design, Philip Farber – Higher Magick, Kendell Geers – Painting My Will, Carl Abrahamsson – The Imaginative Libido, Angela Edwards – The Sacred Whore, Vera Nikolich – The Women of the Aeon, Jason Louv – Wilhelm Reich, Kasper Opstrup – To Make It Happen, Peter Grey – A Manifesto of Apocalyptic Witchcraft, Timothy O'Neill – The Gospel of Cosmic Terror, Stephen Sennitt – Sentient Absence, Carl Abrahamsson – Anton LaVey, Magical Innovator, Alexander Nym – Magicians: Evolutionary Agents or Regressive Twats?, Antti P Balk – Thelema, Kjetil Fjell – The Vindication of Thelema, Derek Seagrief – Exploring Past Lives, Sandy Robertson – The Fictional Aleister Crowley, Adam Rostoker – Whence Came the Stranger?, Emory Cranston – A Preface to the Scented Garden, Manon Hedenborg-White – Erotic Submission to the Divine, Carl Abrahamsson – What Remains for the Future?, Frater Achad – Living In the Sunlight, Genesis Breyer P-Orridge – Magick Squares and Future Beats

The Fenris Wolf 6 (2013)

Carl Abrahamsson – Editor's Introduction, Frater Achad – A Litany of Ra, Kendell Geers – Tripping over Darwin's Hangover, Vera Nikolich – Eastern Connections, Carl Abrahamsson – Babalon, Freya Aswynn – On the Influence of Odin, Marita – Runic Magic through the Odinic Dialectic, Aki Cederberg – Afterword: The River of Story, Shri Gurudev Mahendranath – The Londinium Temple Strain, Gary Dickinson – An Orient Pearl, Derek Seagrief – Aleister Crowley's Birth & Death Horoscopes, Tim O'Neill – Shades of Void, Nema – Magickal Healing, Nema – A Greater Feast, Philip Farber – Sacred Smoke, Robert Taylor – Death & the Psychedelic Experience, Michael Horowitz – LSD: the Antidote to Everything, Alexander Nym – Transcendence as an Operative Category…, Carl Abrahamsson – Approaching the Approaching, Renata Wieczorek – The Secret Book of the Tatra Mountains, Sasha Chaitow – Legends of the Fall Retold, Sara George & Carl Abrahamsson – Sulamith Wülfing, Robert C Morgan – Hans Bellmer, Genesis Breyer P-Orridge – Tagged for Life, Carl Abrahamsson – Go Forth and Let Your Brain-halves Procreate, Anders Lundgren – Satanic Cinema is Alive and Well, Anton LaVey – Appendices

The Fenris Wolf 5 (2012)

Carl Abrahamsson – Editor's Introduction, Jason Louv – The Freedom of Imagination Act, Patrick Lundborg – Such Stuff as Dreams are Made of, Gary Lachman – Secret Societies and the Modern World, Tim O'Neill – The War of the Owl and the Pelican, Dianus del Bosco Sacro – The Great Rite, Philip H Farber – Entities in the Brain, Aki Cederberg – At the Well of Initiation, Renata, Wieczorek – The Magical Life of Derek Jarman, Genesis Breyer P-Orridge – A Dark Room of Desire, Genesis Breyer P-Orridge – Kreeme Horne, Ezra Pound – Translator's Postscript, Stephen Ellis – Poems for The Fenris Wolf, Hiram Corso – Mel Lyman, Mel Lyman – Plea for Courage, Gary Dickinson – The Daughter of Astrology, Robert Podgurski – Sigils and Extra Dimensionality, Frater Nigris – Liber Al As-if, Peter Grey – The Abbey Must be Built, Vera Mladenovska Nikolich – A Different Perspective of the Undead, Kevin Slaughter – The Great Satan, Lionel Snell – The Art of Evil, Phenex Apollonius – The Quintessence of Daimonic Ipseity, Phanes Apollonius – Infernal Diabolism in Theory and Practice, Anonymous – Falling with Love: Embracing the Infernal Host, Lana Krieg – Sympathy with the Devil: Faust's Infernal Formula, Carl Abrahamsson – State of the Art: Birthpangs of a Mega-Golem, Carl Abrahamsson – Hounded by the Dogs of Reason

Also Available From Trapart Books

***The Fenris Wolf 4* (2011)**

Carl Abrahamsson – The whys of yesterday are the why-nots of today, Hermann Hesse – The Execution, Fredrik Söderberg – Black and White Meditations 1-23, Peter Gilmore – Every Man and Woman Is a Star, Peter Grey – Barbarians at the Gates, John Duncan – Hallelujah, Ramsey Dukes – Democracy Is Dying of AIDS, Tim O'Neill – The Technology of Civilization X, Thomas Karlsson – Religion and Science, David Beth – Bloodsongs, Payam Nabarz – Liber Astrum, Hiram Corso – Unveiling the Mysteries of the Process Church, Jean-Pierre Turmel – The Pantheon of Genesis Breyer P-Orridge, Kendell Geers – The Penis Might Ier Than Thes Word, Z'EV – The Calls, Robert Taylor – Dreamachine: The Alchemy of Light, Phil Farber – An Interview with Terence McKenna, Phil Farber – McKenna, Ramachandran and the Orgy, Thomas Bey William Bailey – The Twilight of Psychedelic America?, Ernst Jünger – LSD Again/Nochmals LSD, Baba Rampuri – The Edge of Indian Spirituality, Aki Cederberg – In Search of Magic Mirrors, Carl Abrahamsson – Thelema and Politics, Carl Abrahamsson – Someone's Messing with the Big Picture, Carl Abrahamsson – An Art of High Intent?, Carl Abrahamsson – A Conversation with Kenneth Anger

***The Fenris Wolf 1-3* (1989-1993-2011)**

Carl Abrahamsson – Editor's Introduction
Carl Abrahamsson – 'Zine und Zeit (2011)

THE FENRIS WOLF 1 (1989)
John Alexander – The Strange Phenomena of the Dream, Helgi Pjeturss – The Nature of Sleep and Dreams, Tim O'Neill – A Dark Storm Rising, Carl Abrahamsson – Inauguration of Kenneth Anger, Carl Abrahamsson – An Interview with Genesis P-Orridge, William S Burroughs – Points of Distinction between Sedative and Consciousness-Expanding Drugs, Carl Abrahamsson – Jayne Mansfield: Satanist, TOPYUS – Television Magick, Anton LaVey – Evangelists vs The New God

THE FENRIS WOLF 2 (1990)
Lionel Snell – The Satan Game, Carl Abrahamsson – In Defence of Satanism, Anton LaVey – The Horns of Dilemma, Genesis P-Orridge – Beyond thee Valley ov Acid, Phauss – Photographs, Jack Stevenson – 15 Voices from God, Jack Stevenson – 18 Fatal Arguments, Tim O'Neill – Art On the Edge of Life, Terence Sellers – To Achieve Death, Stein Jarving – Choice and Process, Tim O'Neill – Under the Sign of Gemini, 93/696 – The Forgotten Ones In Magick, Tim O'Neill – The Mechanics of Maya, Coyote 12 – The Thin Line, Genesis P-Orridge – Thee Only Language Is Light, Jack Stevenson – Porno on Film, Carl Abrahamsson – An Interview with Kenneth Anger

THE FENRIS WOLF 3 (1993)
Jack Stevenson – Vandals, Vikings and Nazis, von Hausswolff & Elggren – Inauguration of two new Kingdoms, Tim O'Neill – A Flame in the Holy Mountain, Frater Tigris – A Preliminary Vision, Carl Abrahamsson – The Demonic Glamour of Cinema, William Heidrick – Some Crowley Sources, Peter H Gilmore – The Rite of Ragnarök, ONA – The Left-Handed Path, Zbigniew Karkowski – The Method Is Science..., Fetish 23 – Demonic Poetry, Ben Kadosh – Lucifer-Hiram, Freya Aswynn – The Northern Magical Tradition, Anton LaVey – Tests, Austin Osman Spare – Anathema of Zos, Rodney Orpheus – Thelemic Morality, Nemo – Recognizing Pseudo-Satanism, Philip Marsh – Pythagoras, Plato and the Hellenes, Terence Sellers – A Few

Outsider Inpatient

Acid Writings, Hymenæus Beta – Harry Smith 1923-1991, Andrew M McKenzie – Outofinto, Beatrice Eggers – Nature: Now, Then and Never

Sir Edward Bulwer Lytton: ***Vril – The Power of the Coming Race***

Sir Edward Bulwer Lytton's cautionary tale of occult super-powers and advanced subterranean cultures have fascinated readers since 1871. Part early science-fiction, part educational tract, part occult romance, Vril keeps spellbinding readers thanks to its wide range of themes and emotions, as well as its thrilling sense of adventure.

A curious man descends into a mountain through a mine and experiences far more than he bargained for. Deep inside the mountain lies a completely different world. Its inhabitants, the Vril-ya, are human-like but physically superior and philosophically more advanced. They live in harmony made possible by their wisdom but also by the powerful and potentially destructive magical energy they call "Vril."

The impressed yet terrified visitor is allowed to stay and learn more about their ancient and advanced culture, something very few visitors have – it seems that all the previous adventurers have been mercilessly disposed of by the Vril-ya...

This edition includes an introductory essay by Swedish author Carl Abrahamsson.

More information can be found at our web site: www.trapart.net

www.ingramcontent.com/pod-product-compliance
Ingram Content Group UK Ltd.
Pitfield, Milton Keynes, MK11 3LW, UK
UKHW041851190726
13854UKWH00002B/831

9 789198 624380